inside
racquetball

inside
racquetball

chuck leve

**photographs by
arthur shay
chuck leve**

HENRY REGNERY COMPANY • CHICAGO

Library of Congress Cataloging in Publication Data

Leve, Chuck.
  Inside racquetball.

  (Inside sports)
  1. Paddleball. I. Title.
GV1017.P17L48   796.34   72-11197

Published by Henry Regnery Company
180 North Michigan Avenue, Chicago, Illinois 60601

Manufactured in the United States of America

Library of Congress Catalog Card Number: 72-11197

International Standard Book Number: 0-8092-8899-0 (cloth)
                                    0-8092-8898-2 (paper)

preface

Racquetball is a relatively new game—only five years old in organized form—that has captured the enthusiasm of physical-fitness-minded people throughout North America.

No one really knows when the first paddleball player swapped his solid wooden paddle for a strung racquet or when a tennis player experimented by shortening his racquet or when an avid handball player tried to hit the ball with a racquet instead of his hand. Yet one does know that the game of racquetball was born from a merger of elements of all these games.

When it first appeared, racquetball was criticized loudly by handball players who disliked the game because it used their handball courts, which were already in high demand. As a result, racquetball was banned from many private clubs, community centers, and YMCAs, where over 95 percent of all handball courts are housed. However, the tremendous appeal of racquetball helped it to endure. By the mid-1960s, the sheer number of racquetball fans and players forced its foes to accept the game and allow it to be played more widely.

What *is* the appeal of racquetball? The answer is simple: Racquetball makes it possible for a person to obtain an enjoyable physical and mental workout without requiring a high degree of skill. The game eliminates the pitfalls of a tennis net, yet insists on the same stamina required for handball. Then, too, because of the shortness of the racquet used in racquetball, the game is even faster paced than squash. Another advantage of racquetball is that it can be played by men and women, boys and girls

—anyone old enough to walk and young enough to run.

This book will take you on an inside tour of racquetball. You'll learn the basics of the game and gain the knowledge that will help make your time on court more profitable in terms of enjoyment and physical well-being. The chapters on offensive and defensive shots will help you advance in your playing skills and improve both your singles and doubles games. You'll learn how to win by studying strategies such as control of center court, taking advantage of your opponent's weak areas, anticipating your opponent's shots, and using the proper court coverage formations in doubles. Finally, you'll learn about the importance of thinking clearly under pressure and believing in your playing ability.

To help you understand the technical terms of the game, a Glossary has been provided at the back of the book. Technical words have been italicized throughout the book, and these can all be found in the Glossary.

As the executive secretary of the International Racquetball Association, I have witnessed the highest levels of racquetball competition. The thrill of seeing players crowned champions and the shared disappointment when champions are dethroned has made the sport of racquetball come alive for me.

Many champion racquetball players have given me valuable information on the techniques of playing the game and on learning advanced racquetball shots. My thanks go to Charles Brumfield, Bill Schmidtke, Craig Finger, Ron Rubenstein, Steve Keeley, and Paul Lawrence.

Inside Racquetball passes the winning tips of champions on to you so that as you begin or advance in the game, you will develop skill and proficiency to help you play better and have more fun.

Chuck Leve

contents

IF YOU HAVE NEVER PLAYED RACQUETBALL . . . the best way to learn is from somebody who knows. Most YMCAs, JCCs, and schools have racquetball classes for beginners to help the novice learn the game. Here Art Michaely, physical director of the Northwest Suburban YMCA in Des Plaines, Illinois, teaches a group of enthusiastic women in one of his weekly sessions.

chapter 1
STARTING OUT

If you've been searching for a sport that will help you get and stay in shape and will sharpen your ability to think quickly and clearly, racquetball is your sport. Racquetball allows the individual player to control the game, more so than participating in large-team sports. The necessary equipment is simple, and the rules are not elaborate or difficult to learn.

If you know how to play handball, you'll have a head start on other beginning racquetball players because racquetball is played on a handball court and has similar rules to handball. But if you've never played handball, don't worry. Racquetball is a sport in which you quickly build your proficiency. Once you learn the fundamentals, the excitement and personal satisfaction you'll obtain from racquetball will hold your interest and help you build endurance. Constant practice will increase your familiarity with the court and will help to increase your understanding of the rules of the game.

WHAT TO WEAR

The uniform for racquetball is quite simple. Men will need gym shoes with good tread on the soles to prevent slipping, sweat socks, athletic supporter, gym shorts, and a T-shirt. Women also should wear gym shoes with good tread, sweat socks, gym shorts, and a shirt or blouse. Many women wear tennis outfits. Your uniform should be white or light in color; many tournament players wear all white. Whatever you wear, just make sure your clothes fit comfortably and don't rub against or bind any part of your body as you move about.

It is recommended that you purchase head and wrist sweatbands and a racquetball glove, especially if you tend to perspire a great deal. The head sweatband will keep your hair and sweat out of your eyes (and off your glasses if you wear them), and the wrist sweatbands and glove will absorb perspiration and keep it from dripping on your hands and making them slippery. Eye guards, constructed of aluminum tubing or

THE STANDARD RACQUETBALL UNIFORM. The most important feature of your clothing is comfort; be sure that nothing you wear restricts your freedom of movement.

plastic, which fit over your eyes and are secured by a band around your head, also should be worn. The force at which a racquetball is driven off a player's racquet or bounced off the court walls and floor make the eye guard an especially vital piece of equipment.

THE BALL

The standard IRA (International Racquetball Association)-approved ball is the *Seamless 558,* which is manufactured by the Seamless Rubber Company. The small black ball is used in all tournaments sanctioned by the IRA.

This standard *live* racquetball is 2½ inches in diameter, weighs approximately 1.4 ounces, and, at 76° F., will bounce 67-72 inches high when dropped from a height of 100 inches. Sometimes a player will discover the ball he has purchased is *dead*; that is, when dropped, the ball hardly bounces off the floor. If you have a dead ball, place it in a sauna or steam room, and it will expand and liven up again. However, the expansion also may split the ball, so placing a dead ball in steam isn't always a good cure.

Racquetballs may be purchased for about $1 and normally will last through ten games.

THE RACQUET

You may find it convenient to rent a racquet while you are learning to play. This will give you an opportunity to learn about different models and to get the feel of various racquets. If you wish to purchase a racquet, you'll find at least four major manufacturers: the General Sportcraft Company, the Marcraft Recreation Corporation, the Ektelon Company, and Leach Industries. These companies make quality racquets ranging in price from $6-$45.

Racquets are constructed with aluminum, fiberglass, or steel frames and wood.

THE BALL. The Seamless 558, approved by the International Racquetball Association.

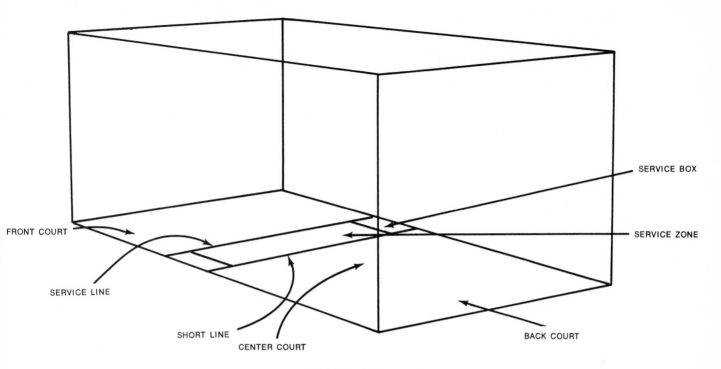

FRONT COURT

SERVICE LINE

SHORT LINE

CENTER COURT

SERVICE BOX

SERVICE ZONE

BACK COURT

DIAGRAM 1. The court.

Although most racquets have nylon strings, gut, monofilament, and metal strings also are available. Nylon strings are probably most preferred and metal least, since metal strings tend to "give" less on impact and thus to decrease the amount of control you have.

According to IRA rules, the racquet *head* must not be more than 9 inches wide or more than 11 inches long. The handle of the racquet must not be more than 7 inches long. The sum of the length and width of the racquet must not exceed 27 inches. IRA rules also require every racquet to have a safety *thong*, a band of string or leather that encircles the player's wrist and secures the racquet to his hand. Be sure you wear the thong whenever you play to insure that your racquet won't fly out of your hand and hit you or your opponent.

Many racquets manufactured today have strips of rubber on the rim of the frame to cushion the edge of the racquet. This prevents damage to the wall and to the racquet when a player accidentally hits the wall.

When you go to buy a racquet, try several brands that you think will be good. Pick up each racquet and swing it a few times, testing its weight and ease of handling. Can you grasp the handle of the racquet firmly and comfortably without crowding or spreading your fingers? Ask the salesperson about the quality and type of string used in the racquet head.

Once you have found a racquet, practice getting used to the feel of it. Remember that while a quality racquet can make a big difference in your game, it never can take the place of learning and mastering the fundamentals.

THE COURT

Racquetball is played on a standard handball court (Diagram 1), 20 feet wide, 40 feet long, and 20 feet high. Though some handball courts have one or three walls, this book will be concerned with four-wall courts. There are five playing surfaces on a court: *front wall, back wall,* two *side walls,* and the *ceiling.* The back wall must be at least 12 feet high and should allow

RACQUETBALL FANS ENJOY . . . watching the drama of the international championships. In this photo Brumfield readies himself for a ceiling shot against Rubenstein in the title match. The glass side walls make it possible for hundreds of spectators to witness top raquetball play.

room for spectator space above. The floor must be wood.

The court walls and ceiling usually are constructed of poured concrete or cement blocks. Courts that use glass in the side and back walls to allow greater visibility for the spectators are available. Prefabricated walls have been introduced recently. They are composed of fiber-resin panels, and they have performed well.

The court is divided by various lines that mark specific playing areas. The *short line* runs parallel to the front wall and divides the court into *front court* and *back court*. The *service line* is 5 feet in front of the

short line and also runs parallel to the front wall. The area between the short line and the service line is the *service zone*. This is the area where the player stands to *serve* the ball. At either end of the service zone, 18 inches from the side wall, are two lines that run parallel to the side walls and define the *service boxes*. In doubles racquetball, the server's partner must stand in one of the service boxes while the ball is being served.

The *receiving lines* are located on each side wall, 5 feet behind the short line. These vertical lines extend 3 inches up the wall and help to give the server some breathing space since the receiver may not cross this line until the ball has been served. Many handball courts are not marked with receiving lines, however. If you play on a court without receiving lines, you and your opponent will have to imagine them.

THE GAME

The complete rules of racquetball appear in Chapter 7. The following general statements will familiarize you with the game.

One player (*server*) stands in the serving zone, bounces the ball in front of him, and hits the ball with his racquet so that it hits the front wall and bounces back anywhere into the court past the short line, with or without hitting one of the side walls. The other player (*receiver*) now must return the ball to the front wall before it bounces on the floor twice. He may hit the ball as it comes off the front wall and before it bounces, or he may hit it after it bounces once on the floor. The receiver then may use any combination of walls or the ceiling to return the ball to the front wall. All shots to be returned must come off the front wall.

If the receiver's return doesn't reach the front wall, or if he can't return his opponent's serve before it hits the floor twice, the receiver loses the *exchange*, and a *point* is awarded to the player who is serving. If the server fails to *return* the ball after the receiver has successfully returned it to the server, the receiver wins the exchange and the right to serve. Only the server can win points. If the server loses an exchange, the receiver only wins the right to serve—not a point.

Game in racquetball is 21 points. There is no *deuce game* in racquetball. The first player to accumulate 21 points wins, even if the score is 21-20.

Once you have hit the ball, no matter whether you are the server or receiver, you must move to allow the other player a clear view and shot at the ball. Failure to move is an *avoidable hinder* and gives your opponent a point if he is serving or the serve if he is receiving. An *unavoidable hinder* is called if one player unavoidably gets in the way of the other player; in this case, the point is replayed. In *club play* you must call your own hinders. In *tournament play*, a referee will decide what type of hinder has occurred and will call it.

Racquetball is played in combinations of two players (*singles*), four players (*doubles*), or three players (*cutthroat* and *one-on-two*). In cutthroat one person serves to the other two players until he loses the volley. He then rotates to a receiving position, and one of the other players becomes the server. One-on-two is a game in which one player plays the other two players throughout the game. The "two" players alternate serving, and the "one" player may get one or two serves, depending on the rules set up between the players.

Singles and doubles racquetball are used in club and tournament play. Cutthroat and one-on-two are not recognized forms of tournament competition and are seen mostly in club play.

Though you may feel now that tournament play is a long way off, a few facts about tournament competition may help you see where you can go with racquetball. The International Racquetball Association divides players into age groups. There are separate men's and women's events both in singles and doubles; there is no competition

RACQUETBALL FOR WOMEN. Throughout the country women are becoming increasingly interested in learning the game. Here Jan Campbell, one of the nation's top female players, demonstrates her skills to a group of women in San Diego.

between men and women, and there is no mixed team play. There are also inter-collegiate competitions and national tournaments for players under nineteen (*Juniors*). The *Masters* singles and doubles events are for men age forty and older. In Masters doubles one player must be at least forty-five years old. There are no Masters events for women at this time.

COURT ETIQUETTE

One important reason for court etiquette in racquetball is to prevent injuries to the players. The racquet, a player's best friend on the court, can become a dangerous weapon when handled carelessly or incorrectly. Then, too, a hard-driven ball can cause serious injury to the unwary player who gets in its way. Though the injured player usually receives the penalty during a game, each player shares equally in the responsibility to learn and to practice the proper playing techniques of the game.

The following guidelines to court etiquette will make racquetball safer and more enjoyable for you and your opponent. By using these guidelines, you'll be a player who is fair to others whether you win or lose.

1. Don't be a wild swinger.—Many beginning racquetball players tend to overswing. This is dangerous and improper technique. As you will learn in Chapter 2, the proper arm motions for most racquetball strokes are short and simple. If you get into the habit of overswinging, you'll find that many players will refuse to play with you.

2. Don't deny your opponent a fair chance to see and return the ball.—Getting

ALL TOP PLAYERS . . . realize the importance of warmup exercises. If you start on the court without loosening up your muscles, you increase your chance of muscle strain. Try to spend 5 or 10 minutes warming up before you play. In the photos on this page Craig Finger does toe touches (*left*) and groin stretches (*right*). On the page opposite Craig demonstrates thigh and calf stretches.

in another player's way is a hinder, which your opponent or the referee will call. Interfering with your opponent's ability to see the ball also is extremely dangerous because you may get hit with his racquet before you can get out of the way.

3. Don't crowd or push your opponent. —Crowding your opponent increases the possibility of your moving into the path of the ball after your opponent hits it and the chance of your getting hit by the racquet. If the ball hits you, your opponent will win the point or the right to serve. Deliberately pushing or shoving the other player is also a point or the serve for your opponent.

4. Don't strike your opponent deliberately.—Racquetball is a game, not a battle. If you feel that you might hit your opponent with the racquet, don't swing. Call a *safety hinder* and replay the point.

WARMUP

Whether you are a beginner or an inter-

national champion, racquetball requires that you be in good condition and ready to do battle on the court. Warmup exercises will help your muscles adapt to the demanding activity of racquetball—the quick stops and starts and hurried lunges.

A racquetball player should spend 5-10 minutes doing warmup exercises before the game. Many players do their exercises in the locker room. You may want to exercise a bit longer than 10 minutes, but don't exercise less than 5 minutes. It's highly unlikely that you will *over*exercise, since empty courts are scarce and you'll want to finish your exercises and get out into the playing area as soon as you can.

Begin by concentrating on relaxing your entire body. Stretch your arms and legs, wiggle and arch your back, and rotate your neck and head. Loosen up as much as you can. Some players jog ¼-½ mile before they play, and this helps their muscles to become supple and loose.

The following exercises will help you warm up for a game or practice session. Take it easy at first, doing only a few of each exercise. Make sure you don't confuse these warmup exercises with the general conditioning exercises described in Chapter 6.

One exercise that you can use to relax the arms is to stand straight with your feet slightly apart and your arms out to your sides, level with your shoulders and parallel to the floor. Keeping your fingers together and hands pointed, make small circles in the air with your arms. You can vary this exercise by making larger circles in the air, by circling both forward and backward with your arms, or by extending both arms straight over your head and making circles.

The second exercise is good for stretching and strengthening your back, stomach, and leg muscles. Sit on the ground with one

RACQUETBALL INVOLVES THE USE . . . of every muscle in your body. Unless you are warmed up properly, you can injure any or all of those muscles. Charlie Brumfield hits what appears to be a routine shot, but countless hours of conditioning have enabled him to do so without injury.

leg fully extended in front of you and the other bent back at the knee and out to the side, not tucked under you. Now lean forward and touch the toes on the extended leg with both hands; alternate legs. With practice, you'll be able to touch your chest to your thighs as you reach forward to touch your toes.

A third warmup exercise is trunk rotation. Stand with your hands on your hips and your feet slightly spread apart. Start by bending from the waist in such a way that your upper body is parallel to the floor. Now lean to the right, back, left, and return to the front position in one continuous swivel motion. Make sure you don't bend your knees as you rotate. This exercise is excellent for improving body flexibility and will increase your ability to move quickly to any position on the court.

The fourth warmup exercise will help you stretch your arms, shoulders, and calf muscles. Stand straight, with your feet flat on the floor and your arms at your sides.

As you rise up on both toes, stretch your playing arm up over your head. In this position, balanced on your toes, go through the motions of unscrewing a lightbulb with your playing hand. When you have the imaginary lightbulb unscrewed, bring your arm down and come down off your toes to a relaxed position. Take several practice swings to warm up the muscles used when you hit the ball.

Your warmup completed, you are ready to step onto the court. Now you can begin to learn and master the fundamentals of racquetball.

TOTAL CONCENTRATION . . . correct form, and proper positioning make a top racquetball player. Here Mike Zeitman, one of the best in the game, readies for a backhand shot against Craig Finger. A split second later Zeitman ended the rally.

chapter 2
FUNDAMENTALS

People of all ages and even entire families play racquetball. The exercise afforded by racquetball keeps a person healthy, and the competition of the game satisfies the aggressive tendencies of all individuals. Above all, racquetball is fun, which accounts for its increasing popularity.

This chapter on fundamentals will help you increase your enjoyment of the game by helping you improve your skills. Mastery of the basic skills described here will help you move on to more advanced skills and help you use your court time more efficiently. In addition, you will learn the importance of coordinating your feet and arm motion, maintaining your balance, and keeping constant eye contact with the ball.

Many of the tips that are included in this chapter have been provided by Charles ("Charlie") Brumfield, 1972 International Singles Champion. Charlie is a champion by virtue of his ability to avoid playing errors and errors in game strategy. He con-

trols each exchange, making his opponent do most of the moving about on the court.

GRIP AND STROKE

Proper *grip* of the racquet and the correct *stroke* are essential for playing good racquetball. Yet because many players don't take enough time to learn the proper grip, they end up not being able to manipulate the racquet and hit the ball where they want it to go.

There are three basic racquetball grips and strokes: *forehand, backhand,* and *overhand.* Descriptions of the strokes given here are for a right-handed player. Left-handed players should substitute "left" for "right" in most instances.

Forehand Grip

To begin the forehand grip, pick up the racquet with your right or left hand, depending on whether you are right-handed or left-handed. Turn the racquet so that the

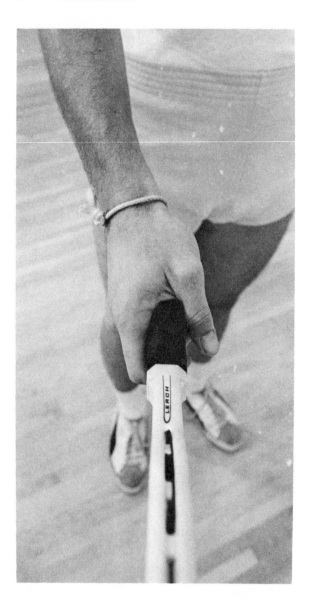

ONE OF THE FIRST SKILLS . . . you will learn in racquetball is the forehand grip, pictured here. The extended "trigger" finger is important for control, and the racquet handle is held securely.

strings are perpendicular, not parallel, to the floor. Now grip the racquet handle as though you were shaking hands with it. You should be able to draw an imaginary line from the racquet frame to the base of the "V" formed by the juncture of your index finger and thumb. Keep your index finger slightly in front of and above your thumb as though you were going to pull the trigger of a gun. Pronounced extension of your index, or "trigger," finger will give you slightly more control in your swing. Curve your fingers around the racquet handle and grip the racquet securely, making sure the end of the handle is set deep into the palm of your hand.

The proper forehand grip allows the player to hit the ball squarely and to send it in a straight line in the desired direction. If you grip the racquet so the racquet face is *closed* (turned slightly toward the floor) or *opened* (turned slightly toward the ceiling) as it makes contact with the ball, your shot will come off the racquet at an up or down angle rather than in a straight line.

THE FOREHAND GRIP. The thumb and forefinger make a V shape, which adds to your ability to balance the racquet and control your shots.

Forehand Stroke

To get into the proper position for the forehand stroke, stand facing the right side wall if you are right-handed, the left side wall if you are left-handed. Grip your racquet in the proper forehand manner; bend your racquet arm slightly at the elbow, and cock your wrist upward. Hold your forearm at a 90° angle to your upper arm and keep your elbow away from your body. Let your free arm hang in a natural manner, straight and relaxed. As you execute the forehand stroke, your free hand will follow the movement of your body naturally. You are now in the *backswing,* or *ready, position* for the forehand stroke.

In game play you should face the front wall with your weight balanced equally on both feet and your eyes on the ball as it comes off the front wall. To execute the forehand stroke, you must pivot your upper body toward the right side wall, lower your right shoulder, and bend your right leg

PERFECT YOUR FOREHAND . . . until it comes naturally. In the pictures on this page Brumfield shows the proper forehand stroke. *Top left*: in the ready position Charlie cocks his arm and wrist. *Top right*: he prepares to make contact with the ball. *Bottom*: he concludes the stroke with the all-important follow-through.

slightly at the knee. Your weight now shifts more onto your right foot, the foot closest to the back wall.

Then you begin to move your lower body toward the front wall and the ball as it comes toward you. At this point, your racquet arm is still bent at the elbow, with your wrist cocked. Your weight now shifts gradually off your right foot as you bring your body and arm around simultaneously until you are putting almost all your weight on your left foot. You should time your swing in such a way that the ball is just off the instep of your left foot, the foot closest to the front wall, when the racquet strikes it.

Don't stop the flowing motion of your lower body as you make contact with the ball. Hit the ball squarely and firmly, with a fully extended arm and an uncocked, not stiff, wrist. As you hit the ball, your arm, wrist, and racquet should form a straight line of power to propel the ball toward the front wall.

Don't stop your arm motion after you hit the ball. Let your arm *follow through* by bending it at the elbow and moving it across your chest and slightly above your left shoulder.

Eventually, with practice, you will be able to calculate mentally the possible returns your opponent may make of your forehand shot. Knowing this, you can immediately move in the direction of his shot *before* he makes it. Your body should be in constant motion, not relaxing even after the hit and follow through. If you stop and start your body, the ball will be returned before you can react, and it will be impossible for you to hit it before it bounces twice on the floor.

A rule of thumb in racquetball is to keep your eyes on the ball at all times, especially as the ball moves into the *hitting area* and makes contact with your racquet.

Charlie Brumfield watches the ball move into the hitting area and then looks at his racquet, maintaining that this technique helps him to judge the ball's distance from the *point of contact*. As Charlie says,

THE BACKHAND GRIP . . . should be perfected because the backhand stroke will be one of your most effective shots. Practice the grip until you can achieve it automatically.

"Once the ball is in the hitting area, you'd better be ready to strike it without hesitating. Otherwise, the ball will get past you, and then you're not going to be able to hit it anywhere."

Backhand Grip

Most players adjust their grip slightly for backhand shots. If you don't, your racquet face will be open (angled upward) when you make contact with the ball. Your shot will then *float*; that is, the ball will come off your racquet face with less force, traveling with less speed and greater height toward the front wall. Your opponent thus will gain additional time to get into position to return the shot.

For the proper backhand grip, grasp the racquet in your right hand in the *handshake grip* you learned for the forehand, with the racquet face perpendicular to the floor. Looking down at the edge of the racquet frame, angle the head of the racquet 2 inches to the right (or left, for left-handers) by turning your wrist. As the racquet head is turned to the right, your hand will slide naturally to the left in order to maintain your grip on the racquet. This slight adjustment of your grip for the backhand stroke allows your racquet to hit the ball squarely, with the face perpendicular to the floor.

The backhand grip may feel a bit unnatural at first. Yet, combined with the proper backhand stroke, this grip will help you make backhand shots efficiently and with maximum power.

Backhand Stroke

To assume the backhand ready position, stand facing the left side wall if you are right-handed, the right side wall if you are left-handed. Your arm should be bent at a 90° angle at the elbow and should be across your midsection toward the left side

of your body (right side if left-handed). Your wrist should be cocked upward, and the top of the racquet frame should be pointed at the back wall. Keep your racquet arm out, away from your body, with your elbow in line with the center of your midsection.

Your feet should be 4-6 inches apart, with your left foot slightly in back of your right foot and parallel with the back wall. Your weight will be on your left foot in the backhand ready position, with your left leg bent slightly at the knee.

As the ball approaches, your weight should shift gradually to your right foot. Some players twist their upper body to the left, toward the back wall, as the ball approaches. However, there is not always time for this added body motion, even though some players find that it gives them more power in their backhand stroke.

Your lower body must turn toward the front wall as you bring your bent arm and cocked wrist into the hitting area. Many players like to bend forward from the waist slightly as they turn toward the front wall. Strike the ball when it passes the instep of your right foot. Straighten your right leg as you shift your weight forward to face the front wall. As in the forehand, make sure you hit the ball squarely, with the racquet face perpendicular to the floor, straightening your arm and wrist after you strike the ball. If your racquet face is not perpendicular to the floor when your racquet crosses your right foot to hit the ball, check to see if you are using the proper backhand grip.

The follow through shouldn't be elaborate or wide-swinging. Just let your backhand arm come around naturally as you pivot your body toward the front wall. Wide "sweeps" of your racquet on the follow through will create a safety hazard for you and your opponent, so they should be avoided.

THE BACKHAND STROKE . . . from approach to follow-through. In the ready position (*top left*) Brumfield bends his arm at a 90° angle. In the next step he shifts his weight forward (*top right*) and prepares to strike the ball (*bottom left*). *Bottom right*: Charlie follows through, and he begins to pivot his body and ready himself for the next shot.

Ideally, your backhand should be as strong as your forehand, thereby challenging your opponent to play anywhere in the court. Yet there are few, if any, players who have equally strong forehand and backhand strokes. Most players find that the backhand requires considerably more time to master and perfect than the forehand. Playing often against more skilled opponents will help develop your backhand because better players will notice if you have a weak backhand and will force you to play it.

Overhand Grip

The overhand grip is the same as the forehand grip except that the player faces the front, not the side, wall to execute an overhand shot. The overhand often is used to retrieve shoulder- or head-high *ceiling balls* or to execute overhand *kill* or *drive shots*. If you can take the ball knee high, however, don't use the overhand stroke; use the backhand or forehand strokes instead.

Overhand Stroke

The overhand ready position is similar to the position you assume to throw a ball. Using the proper grip, stand facing the front wall, with your feet slightly apart and your weight evenly balanced on both feet. Your right arm should be brought back slightly behind your body over your right shoulder. Make sure your forearm is bent at the elbow, forming a 90° angle with the upper arm. Your wrist should be cocked back slightly.

As the ball approaches, shift your weight back slightly, moving your right foot toward the back wall and bending your knees a little. As the ball comes into the hitting area, about 1 foot in front of your body, swing your arm while shifting your weight forward to your left foot. Make contact with the ball by bringing your rac- quet face straight down, in line with your right foot. Hit the ball with the racquet face almost parallel to the front wall, uncocking your wrist at the moment of contact to put full power behind the ball as you let your weight flow forward naturally. Follow through by letting your arm straighten and come down across your body toward your left knee.

When completed, the overhand shot leaves the player in a somewhat awkward position, with his racquet arm extended across his body and his weight on his left foot. A really forceful overhand shot may turn the player's body toward the side wall, leaving him all tied up and out of position to watch the ball as it is returned to him.

The overhand shot is an effective change of pace weapon in racquetball, but it is the least controllable of the three strokes. For this reason, it is best to use the overhand only to hit or retrieve *ceiling shots* or when you can't take the ball knee high (see Chapter 5).

FOOTWORK

An effective forehand, backhand, or overhand shot requires that the player constantly concentrate on the position and movement of his feet. Many tournament players who hit the ball with great skill and coordinate their hands and eyes effectively often use sloppy footwork. Despite the fact that they are off-balance, these players somehow manage to return their opponents' shots with skill and power. Because some tournament players consistently win games despite poor footwork, proper form is forgotten altogether. Yet these players would be even better if they used proper footwork.

No matter what shot you are executing —forehand, backhand, or overhand—your feet never should be separated more than the width of your shoulders when you are

THE OVERHAND STROKE . . . is the least controllable of the three strokes because the off-balance stance required is awkward. You won't use it often during a game — usually only to hit or retrieve ceiling shots.

in the ready position. Ideally your feet will be 4-6 inches apart. A good player keeps his body weight moving—toward the ball as it approaches and toward the front wall as the ball is hit. Thus, the foot that is closest to the front wall receives most of the player's weight at the completion of a shot.

When your opponent hits the ball, you should try to determine where it is likely to land. If you don't move fast enough to the position on the court where the ball is likely to land as it comes off the wall, you will be rushed to get into the backswing for the return. The ball will be past you before you can hit it squarely with the full power of your arm and wrist. By getting into position before the ball comes into the hitting area, you will be able to hit the ball

A BAD PLACE TO BE. Steve Keeley is caught in a terrible court position, having to take a deep-court over-the-head return of a well-placed shot by Paul Lawrence. Lawrence, who has center court position, is looking over his shoulder to see where Steve will return the ball. Always keep your eye on the ball and try to second-guess your opponent.

squarely with the full face of your racquet. If you are not in position, you probably will hit the ball with the racquet face angled upward; this will cause the shot to go high on the front wall, an easy ball for your opponent to retrieve.

BACK WALL TECHNIQUE

Most beginning racquetball players hesitate to use the back wall of the court. Many of them hit the ball while it is still in the air with an overhand shot before it reaches the back wall. As you improve your skills in racquetball, you will learn to use the back wall to your advantage.

A good rule to remember is never to take a ball out of the air when you can play it off the back wall. Once you see that the ball is going to strike the back wall, check to see where your opponent is standing on the court. If he is off to one side of the court, it may be best to pick the ball out of the air and drive it overhand to his opposite side. If your opponent is dominating center court, position yourself facing the side, not back, wall at the place on the court where you think the ball will rebound when it

THIS ACTION SHOT . . . shows several important racquetball skills. Keeley (shooting) takes a backhand off the back wall. Note the intense concentration and eye contact as well as the perfect grip and cocked arm. Paul Lawrence, in center court, watches closely to see where Keeley will hit the ball.

comes off the back wall. Get behind the ball, letting it drop to knee level before you attempt to return it with a forehand or backhand stroke. Don't rush your shot, even if the ball bounces once before it hits the back wall and looks as though it *might* be very close to the floor on its rebound from the back wall. Let the ball come into the proper hitting area before you strike it.

When you take a ball off the back wall, keep an eye on your opponent's court posi-

tion, and make your return a shot that he will find difficult to retrieve. If your opponent is standing in back court behind the receiving line, hit the ball toward the lower right or left corner of front court. If your opponent is in front court, hit the ball with enough force so that it rebounds off the front wall and goes behind your opponent before he can react. But don't strike the ball so hard that it rebounds off the front wall and hits the back wall again or your opponent will be able to recover and set up for the return, and you will have lost your advantage.

If you are truly determined to learn racquetball, you must practice the fundamentals of the forehand, backhand, and overhand strokes and the technique of taking the ball off the back wall. You must practice constantly if you hope to play the game with a satisfactory degree of proficiency. Charlie Brumfield learned racquetball when he was eighteen years old. He practiced five hours a day, every day, hitting hundreds of shots. It's no wonder that he has turned out to be an international champion.

If you play racquetball mainly for fun and exercise, you probably won't want to practice five hours a day. The point is that the amount of practice, both alone and during competition, is directly related to the rate of improvement of your playing skills. The saying, "Practice makes perfect," certainly applies to racquetball.

THE QUARTERS CAN GET CLOSE . . . and the action fast in racquetball, especially in doubles. Each player on the court tries for the best possible position. As Charlie Brumfield races after a well-placed shot, Bill Schmidtke moves out of Brumfield's way and back toward center court, already occupied by Steve Keeley and Craig Finger. Control of the center court position will enable you to hold on to the serve and thus to score points.

chapter 3
SERVE AND SERVE RETURN

In racquetball the player who has the serve has the advantage. The server is the only player who can score points during the volley. A good server plans his serve carefully and takes full advantage of his mid-court position to put his opponent in the worst possible situation.

The *serve return* is also an important factor in determining the winner of the game. Practice and concentration on the proper serve return will prevent you from missing your serve return attempts and will reduce your chances of continually losing games by a slim margin. Often a player loses a game through his over-eagerness to attempt difficult kill shot returns instead of making safer offensive shots.

The serve and the serve return are the most important shots in racquetball. If you learn the proper fundamentals of the serve and serve return and practice them constantly, you'll be well on your way to becoming a better player.

SERVE

The mid-court serving position (Diagram 2) gives the server an advantage. He can move more quickly and directly to any position on the court for the return, remembering, of course, to keep his eye on his opponent and the ball at all times. When you're serving, don't lose the serve and your advantage by being inattentive for even a second.

To serve the ball, you *must* bounce it on the floor within the service zone at least once, but no more than three times. You may serve from any place in the service zone, but you must stand with both feet within the service zone as you strike the ball. The served ball must then hit the front wall and go past the short line to any position on the court. The ball may hit one of the side walls, but if it hits *two* side walls after hitting the front wall, it is considered a *fault*. (See Rule 4.5 in Chapter 7.)

After you serve the ball, watch your op-

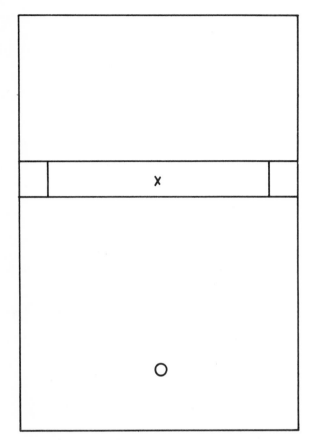

DIAGRAM 2. Server and receiver in singles.

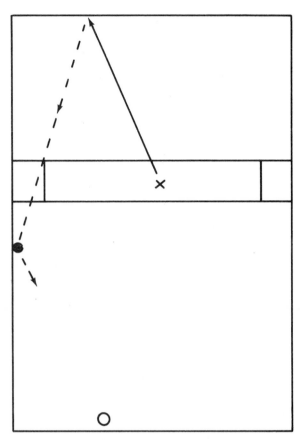

DIAGRAM 3. The drive serve.

ponent retrieve and strike it. Don't stand facing the front wall, back wall, or your opponent. By simply peeking over your right or left shoulder, you'll be able to see where your opponent is striking the ball. Keep moving and anticipating your opponent's return shots.

The server wins a point and the right to continue serving when his opponent fails to return the ball before it hits the floor twice. The server loses the serve when he fails to return his opponent's shot or when he commits an avoidable hinder. Loss of serve is an *out,* sometimes called a *hand-out.*

There are three basic serves in racquetball: the *drive serve,* the *lob serve,* and the *cross-court serve.* The *reverse cross-court serve (Garfinkel)* is a variation of the cross-court serve. The effect of your serve will vary depending on whether you use a forehand, backhand, or overhand stroke and where you stand in the service zone.

Most players feel more confident using the forehand stroke to serve since the backhand and overhand strokes normally give a player less control of the ball.

Drive Serve

The drive serve (Diagram 3) is the most common serve in racquetball. The term "drive" may bring to mind a hard-hit ball, yet it is also a ball that hits the front wall and rebounds in a straight line, without the use of any of the other walls. When hit correctly, the drive serve is an *ace*—a serve that is impossible for the receiver to return, which results in a point for the server.

To execute the drive serve, stand near the middle of the service zone and face the right side wall. Hold the racquet in the prop-

THE DRIVE SERVE. This shot, very well carried out by Craig Finger, is struck at about knee level. Craig's footwork is properly coordinated with the rest of his body, the racquet, and the ball.

er forehand ready position, with your weight shifted slightly back on your right foot and the ball in your left hand. Now bounce the ball on the floor about a racquet's length in front of you and begin to pivot your lower body forward onto your left foot, shifting your weight forward in a flowing motion. Pivot your body so that your racquet comes into the hitting area as the ball bounces up into the air. Hit the ball at knee level or slightly higher.

If hit correctly, a drive serve will hit the front wall and land in two possible places: low on the side wall just behind the short line in the *crotch* (point where any two court surfaces join), or low and deep into the *backhand corner* of the court. The first area, low on the side wall, is especially effective when your opponent is playing in *deep court* or if your opponent is expecting you to serve the ball with a soft touch. When you hit the ball into the second area, the deep backhand corner, your opponent will have to rush to set up and retrieve it.

Use the drive serve cautiously, however. If you serve the ball so hard that it rebounds high on the side wall, the ball will come off the side wall and rebound to the back wall, giving your opponent time to set up for the return. If your opponent is expecting you to use a hard drive serve, he will get in position to kill the low serve or hit an effective pass shot on either side of the court.

A variation of the drive serve is the *three-quarter speed* (or *off-speed*) *drive* (Diagram 4). This type of serve, hit more softly than a hard drive, is often very difficult to return since the receiver believes he has been set up for a kill return. The ball is

hit into deep court, where it begins to slow down. The receiver, overanxious to kill the shot before it drops to the floor, miscalculates his return, and the ball drops short of the front wall.

Lob Serve

The lob serve (Diagram 5) is used often by many of the nation's top players. When correctly executed, the lob serve is a softly hit, low-speed shot to the side of the court opposite the server.

When using the lob serve, stand slightly off-center in the service zone. If you want the ball to land in left court, stand off-center to the right. For a right court shot, stand off-center to the left.

Choosing the exact spot on the front wall where you want the ball to hit and

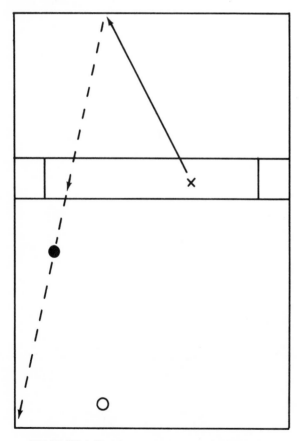

DIAGRAM 4. The three-quarter speed drive serve.

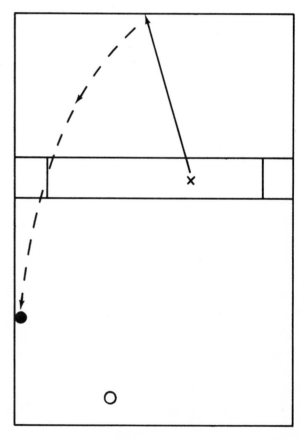

DIAGRAM 5. The lob serve.

THE LOB SERVE. Craig Finger uses his entire body to give this soft shot extra oomph. Properly done, the lob can be very effective, but you run the risk of giving your opponent a perfect set up.

using the proper forehand stroke, hit (don't push) the ball hard enough so that it hits the front wall and rebounds onto the side wall high and deep (about 7-8 feet from the back wall). A lob serve will spin slowly after its impact with the front and side walls and will tend to slow down as it drops in or near your opponent's backhand corner. A proper lob serve must rebound off the front wall onto the side wall. If it does not hit the side wall, your opponent will rush up into mid-court, take the ball out of the air, and smash it past you. Also, a lob serve that doesn't hit the side wall won't slow down enough and may even hit the back wall, giving your opponent a perfect setup and plenty of time to choose his return shot.

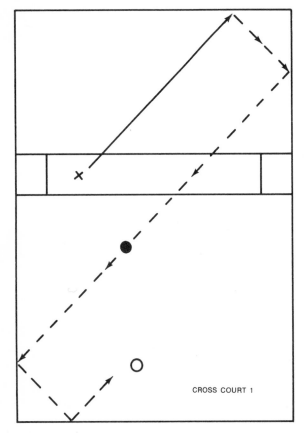

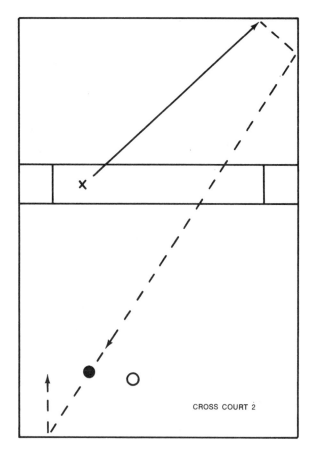

DIAGRAM 6. The cross-court (scotch or Z) serve.

Cross-Court Serve

In the cross-court serve (Diagram 6)—also called *scotch* or *Z serve*—the server uses a forehand stroke to hit the ball to the front wall near the crotch so that it rebounds sharply onto the side wall and bounces deep into the receiver's backhand corner.

Execute a cross-court serve from a slightly off-center serving position. If you serve off-center, you have a better angle of delivery, and the receiver won't be able to determine whether the ball will rebound to the back wall or deep opposite the side wall. The receiver who tries to anticipate where the ball will rebound usually makes the wrong choice and gets in a court position that results in an ineffective return.

When you use the cross-court serve, be careful not to hit the side wall or ceiling first, rather than the front wall. This is an illegal, *nonfront serve,* which results in an out. Another pitfall of the cross-court serve is the *three-wall serve*—a serve that hits three walls before it strikes the floor. The penalty for a three-wall serve is a fault, and two faults in succession are an out.

Reverse Cross-Court Serve (Garfinkel)

The reverse cross-court serve—Garfinkel —(Diagram 7) is a variation of the cross-court serve hit to your opponent's forehand. The serve is named after Charlie Garfinkel, the first player to use this serve in international competition.

To execute the Garfinkel serve, stand slightly to the right of center in the serving zone. Using the forehand stroke, hit the ball with medium-hard firmness toward the left front wall near the crotch. The

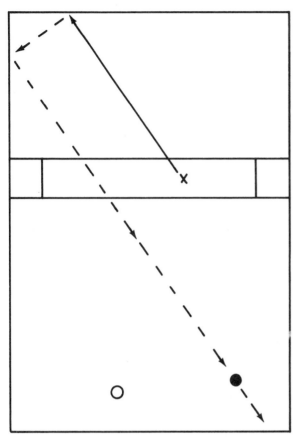

DIAGRAM 7. The reverse cross-court (Garfinkel) serve.

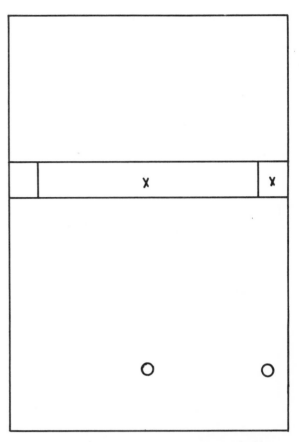

DIAGRAM 8. Server, partner, and receiver in doubles.

ball will rebound at a sharp angle off the front wall and will land deep in your opponent's forehand corner.

Since the forehand area of the court is normally a player's strongest hitting area, the Garfinkel serve is admittedly more of a gamble than other serves. If you execute a Garfinkel serve expertly, however, your opponent will attempt a kill return off a ball too high to be killed effectively. If this occurs, you will have challenged your opponent on something he thought he could do quite well. This disturbing fact may cause him to lose a bit of that all-important concentration.

Yet even if your opponent does manage to return your Garfinkel serve, his return is not likely to be an effective one. If the receiver is standing close to the back wall, he won't be able to extend his arm high

enough to return the ball offensively. A kill shot return is quite ineffective on such a high and deep serve as the Garfinkel.

The Garfinkel must be perfected before it is tried since there is little margin for error when you use it. Always keep in mind that you are playing into your opponent's strength. A weak Garfinkel usually will be returned, and you may lose your serve.

Doubles Serve

Doubles players first must decide which players will be partners. Sometimes a right-handed player will pair up with a left-handed player so neither will have to play his backhand. Whenever two right-handed players pair up, the more skillful backhand player plays the left side of the court.

The serve in doubles (Diagram 8), as in singles, is the most important shot in a volley. To serve, the server stands within the service zone. His partner must stand in the service box with his back to the side wall and must not leave the service box until the served ball has passed the short line.

The drive and cross-court serves are very effective in doubles. Lob serves are used occasionally but are slower and easier for your opponent to retrieve. Also, a poorly hit lob serve invites your opponent to strike it on the fly, perilously close to your partner.

Serving Tips

The complete serving rules are listed in Chapter 7. The following are general tips based on the rules, and you should keep them in mind when practicing your serve.

1. After the server bounces the ball, he must hit it directly to the front wall. If the ball strikes any other surface first, it is a nonfront serve and an out.

2. After the ball strikes the front wall, it must not strike the server on the rebound. If the server gets hit with the ball while it is in the air, he loses his serve.

3. In doubles, if a served ball hits the server's partner in the serving box, it is a dead ball and must be replayed.

4. A served ball that hits the floor in front of the short line is a *short serve* and a fault.

5. A served ball that strikes the back wall without hitting the floor first is a *long serve* and a fault.

6. A served ball that strikes the front wall and then the ceiling is a *ceiling serve* and a fault.

7. A served ball that hits the front wall and rebounds, hitting two side walls on the fly, is a three-wall serve and a fault.

8. A *foot fault* is committed when the server steps beyond the service line when serving or when, in doubles, his partner steps beyond the service box before the served ball passes the short line.

9. The server who commits two faults in a row loses the serve.

SERVE RETURN

An effective return of the serve is essential in racquetball because it determines whether you give up a point or whether you gain the serve and the opportunity to score. As the receiver, you are on the defensive. You want to regain the center-court position and the serve.

After the ball is served, the receiver must hit the ball back to the front wall before it hits the floor twice. You may hit the ball in the air (on the fly) or after it bounces once. If the ball bounces on the floor again on its way to the front wall, the receiver loses the *rally*. The action stops, and the server serves the ball again for the next point.

The receiver may return the ball directly to the front wall. More often, however, he uses one or both side walls, the back wall, the ceiling, or any combination of these surfaces to return the ball to the front wall.

Many players use both hands to hold the racquet and strike the ball. However, this is a matter of preference. Use one or both hands on the racquet but don't switch the racquet from hand to hand at any time or you will lose the volley, and the server will get the point.

If you swing at the ball and miss, you have not automatically lost the point. If you can recover quickly enough from your original miss and still return the ball before it hits the floor, you are okay.

An ineffective serve return gives your opponent the advantage. Practicing effective serve returns will enable you to survive what is often the worst of the battle on the court.

A player may use any of the basic strokes to return serves. Keep in mind, however,

THE DRIVE RETURN. Paul Lawrence demonstrates the steps of the fluid movement from ready position to backhand return.

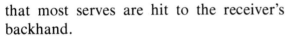

that most serves are hit to the receiver's backhand.

The type of serve return you use depends on the type of serve you receive. There are six basic serve returns: the *drive return*, the *ceiling return*, the *lob return*, the *kill return*, the *Z ball return*, and the *around-the-wall return*. Skillful execution of these serve returns will greatly improve your ability to win games.

Drive Return

The drive return (Diagram 9 and 10) is most successful when used to return a drive serve. The ball already is traveling at a high rate of speed so that a drive return will give even greater speed and force to the ball, moving the ball past the server before he can react. If your opponent is slowing down the game by using three-quarter speed drive or lob serves, a good,

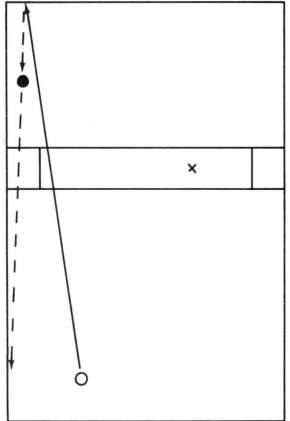

DIAGRAM 9. The down-the-line drive return.

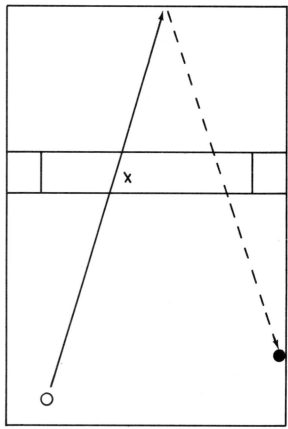

DIAGRAM 10. The cross-court drive return.

hard drive return will quicken the pace of the game enormously.

There are two possible drive returns that the receiver may use: the *down-the-line drive return* and the *cross-court drive return*. In the down-the-line drive return, as the ball comes into the backhand hitting area, use the backhand stroke to hit the ball squarely and forcefully in a straight line to the left front wall so that it rebounds deep into the backhand corner. Some players angle the ball slightly toward the left side wall, yet sometimes this is not a good technique. If the ball hits the side wall at too sharp an angle, it may bounce out into mid-court. Otherwise, if the server is in mid-court, and the server will be able to pick the ball out of the air.

The drive return also may be hit cross-court. This variation of the regular drive return is particularly good when the server

is not in mid-court. Otherwise, if the server is in mid-court, as he should be, he will be in a perfect position to step into the path of the ball and kill it.

To execute the cross-court drive return, you must use your strongest backhand stroke to hit the ball on an angle to the right front wall so that it comes off the wall and carries into the deep forehand corner. If you hit the ball to the front wall at too wide an angle, it will hit the side wall and bounce into mid-court, where the server will pick it off. If you hit the ball to the front wall at too narrow an angle, it will rebound directly to the server in mid-court. Never hit a drive return above knee or thigh level on the front wall. A drive return that is hit too high on the front wall will carry to the back wall and give the server a perfect setup.

Use the drive return to catch the server off-guard. If he always serves from one side of the service zone, use a drive return to the opposite side of the court.

Ceiling Return

Probably the most common serve return used today by tournament players is the ceiling return (Diagram 11). It is used primarily to return lob, three-quarter, or Garfinkel serves. When you can't kill the ball, the ceiling return is your best defensive shot.

The ceiling return is a medium-hard shot hit with the face of the racquet angled upward so that the ball strikes the ceiling about 2 feet in front of the front wall, drops down to the front wall, rebounds out into the court near the short line, and dies near the back corner of the court.

A variation of the straight ceiling return is the *front-wall-first ceiling return*—a shot in which the ball hits the front wall first, about 2 feet below the ceiling, and then rebounds onto the ceiling and drops into back court. This variation is especially good when the server is close to the front wall in *short court*.

As with all serve returns, however, if poorly executed, the ceiling return will give your opponent an excellent setup. If you hit the ball too softly, the ball will not carry deep enough, and your opponent will hit

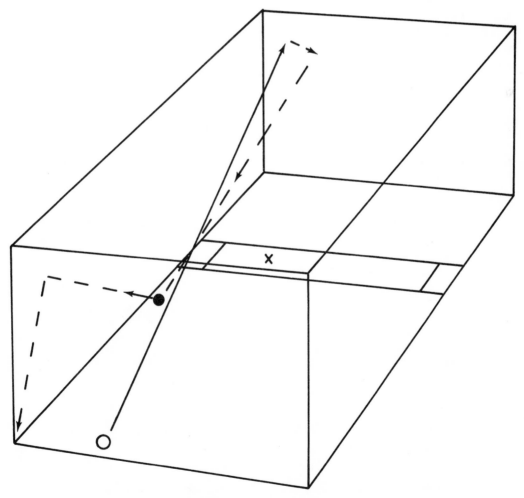

DIAGRAM 11. The ceiling return.

THE MOST COMMON SERVE RETURN . . . in racquet-ball today is the ceiling ball. Keeley strokes the back-hand ceiling ball: he strides into the ball (*top left*) and hits it at about chest height. Steve's arm is fully extended as he hits. *Bottom*: Keeley follows through to complete the shot.

the ball from front court. If you hit a ceiling return too hard, the ball will come off the back wall for the setup.

The ideal ceiling return is a *wallpaper ball*—a ball that clings to the side wall as it drops down in deep court.

A well-hit ceiling return will bring the server out of his advantageous center-court position. Also, a ceiling ball usually can't be returned with anything but another ceiling ball. Thus a good ceiling ball seldom will be killed by the server.

Lob Return

Once the most frequently used return in the game, the lob return (Diagram 12) has dropped off considerably since 1971 with the invention of the live racquetball. The newer balls bounce higher than the original

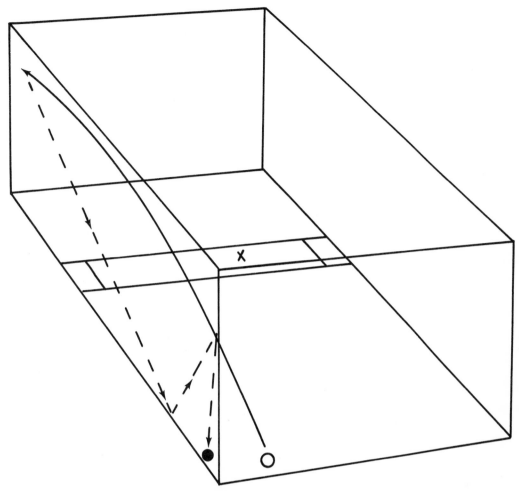

DIAGRAM 12. The lob return.

ones and are more challenging to control. Though still considered an effective return shot, the lob has been replaced primarily by the ceiling return.

The lob may be used effectively to return any type of serve. It is a good defensive shot because it moves the server out of center court and allows you to regain the position.

The lob return is hit with a soft backhand from left back court. The ball should hit high on the left front wall and hug the left side wall behind the short line as it bounces on the floor and drops down into the deep backhand corner. If your lob return does not strike or scrape the side wall, it will not slow down in time to avoid hitting the back wall for the setup.

A proper lob return will not hit the ceiling or the back wall. Do not attempt to hit a cross-court lob return; the ball has to travel so far so slowly that your chances of making an effective shot are very slim.

The difficult, delicate nature of the lob return is best summed up by Charlie Brumfield: "When I can't do anything else, I'll lob."

Kill Return

The kill return (Diagram 13) is one of the more difficult serve returns to execute properly. A good kill return will strike the front wall so low that the server will not be able to get to the ball before it rolls on the floor. The ideal kill return is the *flat rollout*, which is a shot that comes off the front

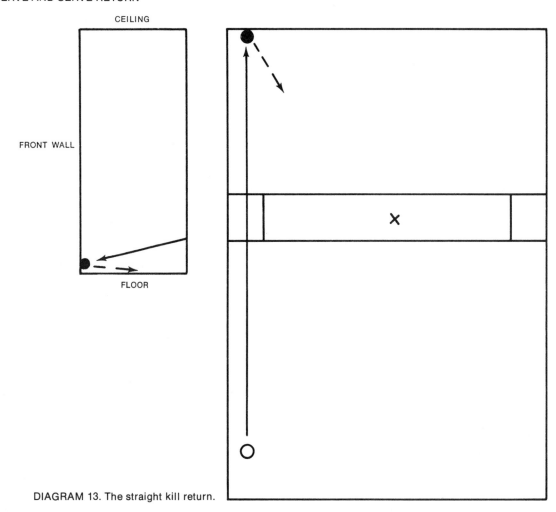

DIAGRAM 13. The straight kill return.

wall so close to the floor that the players barely can see it bounce.

The best opportunity to use the kill return is provided by a hard-hit serve that comes off the back wall in a setup. The kill return also is used to return any poorly executed serve.

Charlie Brumfield estimates that he attempts approximately one kill return out of every ten balls served to him, "just to keep 'em guessing." His cautious attitude is undoubtedly due to the fact that a kill return is a low-percentage shot—the server is in the optimum retrieving position. If the server anticipates a kill shot, he can return it easily. Since the ball must be returned to the front wall first, it is a *skip-in*, or *skip*, ball and gives the server a point.

Z Ball Return

The Z ball (Diagram 14) is extremely effective but is also the most difficult of all the returns to hit correctly. A player must have a great deal of strength and pinpoint accuracy to hit a good Z ball return.

The receiver stands in deep left court and strikes the ball backhand to the right front wall near the side wall crotch. If the Z ball return is hit high and hard enough, it will angle to the right side wall, rebound to the left side wall in deep court, and come off parallel to the back wall. An ideal Z ball return will rebound so close to the back wall that the server will find it impossible to return the ball. A proper Z ball return never should hit the ceiling because the ceiling will slow it down and make the ball

THE FOREHAND KILL . . . is shown here by Bill Schmidtke. The ball is struck when it is close to the ground, off the instep of the front foot. This shot can be used as a serve return if the serve is a set up. The forehand kill is a difficult shot, but Schmidtke does it perfectly.

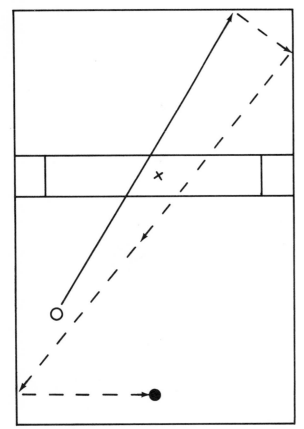

DIAGRAM 14. The Z ball return.

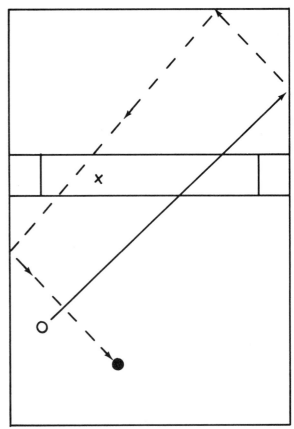

DIAGRAM 15. The around-the-wall return.

drop in mid-court after it comes off the side wall.

The Z ball return is best used to retrieve lob, scotch, or Garfinkel serves.

Around-the-Wall Return

The around-the-wall return (Diagram 15) is similar to the Z ball but much easier to hit. Like the Z ball, it is used to return lob, scotch, or Garfinkel serves.

The receiver stands in left court behind the short line. The ball is hit backhand to a point on the right side wall. The ball then rebounds on a sharp angle to the front wall, comes off the front wall, and angles toward the left wall, striking the floor at three-quarter court.

Like any good defensive serve return, the around-the-wall return moves the server out of center court and gives you the advantage.

Doubles Serve Return

The objective of the serve return in doubles is to force one or both opponents out of center court. This can be accomplished most effectively by using the ceiling or Z ball return.

In doubles it is usually a mistake to attempt to kill the ball on a serve return. A receiver in deep court has the opposing team in front of him when he attempts to kill the ball. If his kill attempt is not perfect, one of the opposing players will find it quite easy to re-kill the ball successfully for the point.

Serve Return Tips

The rules regarding serve returns are listed in Chapter 7. If followed carefully, these general tips based on the rules will improve your serve return while you are learning the game.

1. When the ball is being served, the receiver must stand at least 5 feet in back of the short line and must not return the ball until it passes the short line.

2. Even if you think the serve was illegal, don't touch the ball until it hits the floor twice.

3. When you hit the ball on the fly as the serve comes off the front wall, don't step into the service zone or you'll lose the volley.

STRENGTH AND PINPOINT ACCURACY . . . are required for the proper execution of the forehand Z ball. In the photographs on this page Steve Keeley shows how it is done. After he completes the shot, he follows through across his body.

THE SHOOTER. The well-known phrase in racquetball circles certainly applies to Steve Keeley. The shooter has enough confidence in his game to attempt kill shots from almost any place on the court. In this case Keeley has chosen to shoot to the front-right corner despite Paul Lawrence's center court position.

chapter 4
OFFENSIVE SHOTS

With practice, you'll find that you can become a satisfactory racquetball player easily and quickly. Becoming an advanced player and a consistent winner, however, takes much more time, energy, and dedication.

The skilled racquetball player knows how to use both the offensive and defensive shots of the game. He is not restricted by his inability to execute shots with precision or by his position on the court. Because a good player is a versatile player, his opponent never knows what his next shot will be.

In this chapter you'll learn to hit the basic offensive shots: *kill shot, drop shot,* and *pass shot*. In addition, you'll receive some helpful tips about how to use these shots from 1971 international champion Bill Schmidtke and top-ranked player Ron Rubenstein.

KILL SHOT

The kill shot in racquetball is comparable to the strikeout in baseball. Like the strike-out, the kill shot ends the action and concludes the play. Yet while even the most expert racquetball player isn't able to kill *every* ball, the player who can't kill *any* ball is in serious trouble.

Any unreturnable shot that hits low on the front wall qualifies as a kill shot. The ultimate kill, the flat roll-out, is impossible to return because a player can't possibly get his racquet under the ball before it hits the floor.

There are two primary risks in executing kill shots. First, a player may hit the ball so low to the front wall that it drops short, hitting the floor before it hits the front wall. Second, a player may hit the ball too high on the front wall. If the ball rebounds into the court, your opponent will retrieve it quite easily.

Despite its pitfalls, a properly hit kill shot is a player's bread and butter. When the opportunity presents itself, a good player moves in quickly with his forehand or backhand kill.

"I CAN'T STRESS ENOUGH . . . the importance of practice," says Ron Rubenstein, one of the best backhand shooters in racquetball. When he demonstrated the backhand kill, Ron's stroke from approach (*top left*) to follow-through (*bottom right*) was too quick for the camera. The point of contact is pictured at bottom left.

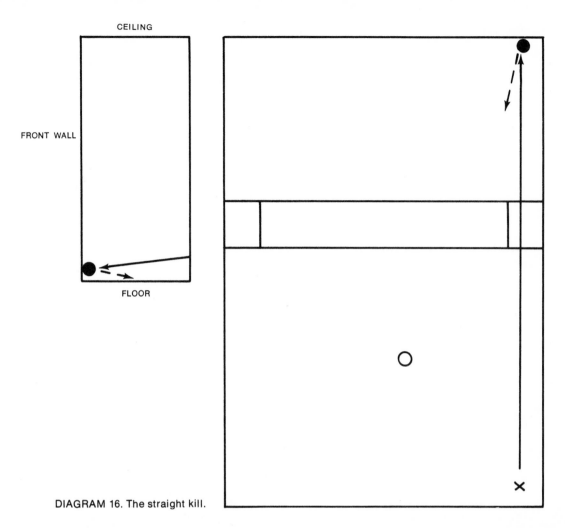

DIAGRAM 16. The straight kill.

Ron Rubenstein is one of the best backhand shooters in racquetball. Ron believes three factors helped him to develop an effective backhand kill: competition, practice with others, and individual practice. "I can't stress enough the importance of practice," he says. "The player should get out on the court and hit backhand kills and other shots over and over again, hour after hour. I got so I could hit kills in my sleep!"

To survive against good competition, every racquetball player should be able to hit a proper forehand and backhand kill. And if you've got tournament competition in mind, you'd better make sure that even your backhand kill is better than "just adequate."

There are four varieties of kill shots in racquetball: *straight, side wall-front wall,* *front wall-side wall*, and *off-the-back wall*. Any of these kill shots may be executed either with the forehand or backhand strokes.

Straight Kill

The straight kill (Diagram 16) is an effective and commonly used kill shot. The player hits the ball straight into the front wall as low as possible. To hit the forehand straight kill, the player must strike the ball at calf level or slightly lower, driving it into the lower right-hand corner of the front wall. The ball will travel almost perfectly parallel to the right side wall and come off the front wall low and along the side wall.

It is very important to hit kill shots at calf, not knee, level or below. "I really get down there," claims Bill Schmidtke. "I bend my back and my knees, reach about a

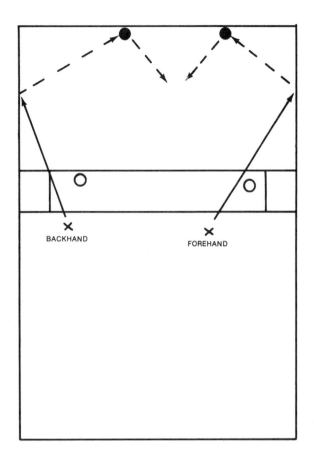

DIAGRAM 17. The side wall-front wall kill.

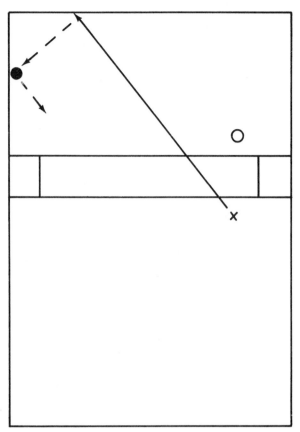

DIAGRAM 18. The front wall-side wall kill.

foot out from my body, and hit the ball slightly more than a racquet's width above the floor. Sometimes I get so low that I actually scrape my hand on the floor."

Bill is a player who is known for his on-the-mark forehand kill shots. In fact, he won the International Singles Championship in 1971 on the strength of his forehand shooting. "If I'm going to win," says Bill, "I need to kill with my forehand. In fact, I've geared my entire game to making my opponent make the mistake that will give me this shot. Then I quickly take advantage of his mistake."

The backhand straight kill is struck even lower than the forehand straight kill. The player uses the backhand stroke to hit the ball low, somewhere between his calf and ankle, just off the instep of the foot that is closest to the front wall, and about 1 foot

away from his body. The ball should be hit directly into the left-hand corner of the front wall.

Tournament players use the straight kill in about 70 percent of all kill shot attempts. Many players prefer the straight kill to other kill shots since the ball strikes only one surface, the front wall.

Side Wall-Front Wall Kill

The second variety of kill shot is the side wall-front wall kill (Diagram 17). The player hits the ball low, with the racquet face opened slightly so the ball strikes the side wall first. When the ball hits the side wall, the ball caroms off so that it moves toward the front wall instead of away from it. Hitting the front wall slows the ball down further and makes it die as it hits the front wall.

"I use the side wall-front wall kill if my opponent is next to or behind me," says Bill Schmidtke. "By the time he reacts to the shot hitting the side wall, it's too late for him to retrieve the ball at the front wall."

The side wall-front wall kill can be hit from anywhere on the court, but it is most effective when you are near either side wall and your opponent is near you. Remember to hit the side wall first or the ball won't die after it hits the front wall.

A tip for beginners: the side wall-front wall kill is especially effective against players who do not watch the ball. If your opponent is not looking at you, the use of the side wall in making kill attempts will be devastating.

Front Wall-Side Wall Kill

The front wall-side wall kill (Diagram 18) is the least common type of kill shot because it has the most pitfalls. It is hit with the basic forehand or backhand stroke to the opposite low corner of the front wall. If the shot is executed properly, the ball then angles into the closest side wall and rebounds off the wall onto the floor.

There are at least two pitfalls to the front wall-side wall kill shot. If, as the ball comes off the side wall, it angles wide, high, and out toward the center of the court, your opponent will have a perfect setup. Or, if the ball hits the floor near the front wall-side wall crotch, it will bounce high and provide a possible setup.

Remember that in the front wall-side wall shot, the ball's path is directed toward center court, exactly where you don't want the ball to go.

"I attempt the front wall-side wall kill only if my opponent is out of position," says Schmidtke. "Otherwise the chances for a setup off a missed shot are just too great."

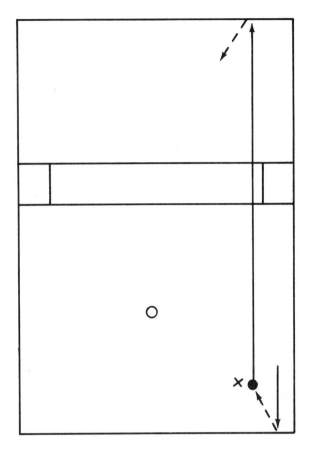

DIAGRAM 19. The off-the-back-wall kill.

Off-the-Back Wall Kill

The off-the-back wall kill (Diagram 19) is used frequently and successfully by many top-ranked racquetball players. The back wall is an added factor that helps give the player ample time to get set up for the shot.

When you see that a shot is going to come off the back wall, you should get into position in the hitting area and wait for the ball to drop low, but not so low that you can't get your racquet under it. Put your full power into your swing as you strike the ball into the lower right front corner, as though you were making a straight kill shot.

"I use the kill about 75 percent of the time when I get a backhand shot off the back wall," says Rubenstein. "I try not to kill it if my opponent is in front court, however."

Most players use the kind of kill shot

BILL SCHMIDTKE PUTS POWER . . . into his swing as he strikes the ball in this off-the-back-wall kill. This can be a very successful shot, so you should practice until you are proficient at it. Footwork is important in making this shot. Notice Bill's weight transfer from back foot (*top right*) to front foot (*bottom left*).

they can hit the best. By practicing and playing, you'll learn which type of kill shot works best in a given situation. When you can analyze a shot quickly, take it, and kill it, you know you're playing good racquetball.

DROP SHOT

The drop shot (Diagram 20) is somewhat like the straight kill because the player hits the ball to only one surface, the front wall, and then waits for it to die. The drop shot is used to strike a ball that has hit near the crotch of the floor and the front wall and then has bounced up. The player stands in front court holding his racquet low, with his wrist cocked back. As the ball bounces out, the player moves up court quickly—like a baseball player catching a ball on the short hop. The player connects with the ball by cocking his wrist forward and hitting the ball softly, out in front of his body. The ball should be angled to the right or left front wall. If hit softly enough, the ball will "drop" into the front wall and hardly rebound.

If hit too hard, the offensive drop shot can be a dangerous shot, easily picked off by your opponent as it rebounds. Also, because the drop shot is a slow, softly hit ball, your opponent will have a bit more time to retrieve it if you haven't angled it quite enough into the left or right side of the front wall.

When hit correctly, however, the drop shot can really surprise your opponent. The slow speed of the shot will be an excellent change of pace ball in a fast-hitting game. To retrieve your drop shot, your opponent often must make an energy-consuming sprint from deep to front court. Even if he gets to the ball before it bounces twice, his setup for the next return will be so rushed that it will be weak and ineffective.

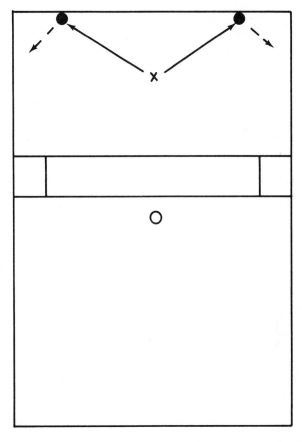

DIAGRAM 20. The drop shot.

With the modern live ball, the drop shot requires a very light touch. Practice your "soft" shots often, and you'll be ready with your drop when your opponent is daydreaming in back court.

PASS SHOT

The pass shot is executed by hitting the ball hard, past your opponent, for a point. It is probably the easiest of the offensive shots because it does not demand pinpoint accuracy. In a good pass shot your opponent can't reach the ball in time and thus wastes his playing energy. A pass is a good shot to use when you see your opponent leaning or moving forward in anticipation of your kill shot. A hard pass shot will be far beyond your opponent before he knows what's happened.

With practice, you'll learn to overcome

THE FOREHAND DROP SHOT . . . is well executed here by Charlie Brumfield. He takes the ball on its way up and drops it in for a kill.

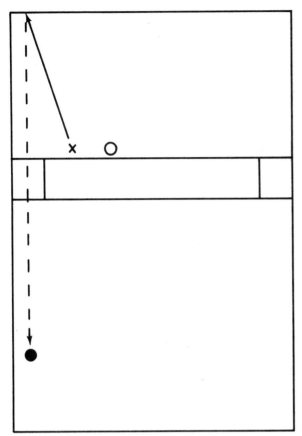

DIAGRAM 21. The down-the-line pass.

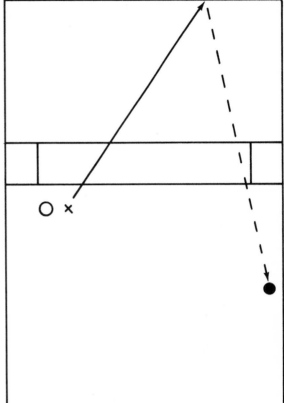

DIAGRAM 22. The cross-court pass.

the tendency to hit the pass shot so hard that it comes off the back wall to provide a setup for your opponent.

There are three types of pass shot: *down-the-line, cross-court*, and *V*.

Down-the-Line Pass

Use the down-the-line pass (Diagram 21) when you are standing in or near center court, with your opponent on your right or left. Keeping your body between the ball and your opponent, hit the ball in a line parallel to the side walls ("down-the-line") opposite your opponent. The ball should hit the front wall about waist or thigh level and rebound into the court without hitting the side wall.

Sometimes, however, the ball will strike the side wall in deep back court on the

rebound. While this is not an incorrect down-the-line pass, it does open up the possibility that the ball will angle off to the back wall and provide a setup for your opponent.

Cross-Court Pass

The cross-court pass (Diagram 22) is a real shock shot, which is best used when your opponent is positioned far to one side of the court near one of the side walls.

The cross-court is stroked forehand or backhand from back court. The ball should hit the front wall at waist or thigh level near or at the midpoint of the wall. The ball will rebound cross-court, opposite your opponent, and into the back corner. Like the down-the-line pass, the cross-court pass must be hit with a light enough touch so

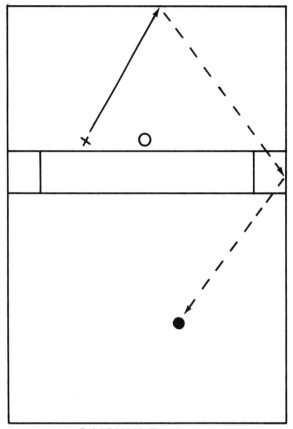

DIAGRAM 23. The V pass.

THE PASS. Brumfield makes a desperate stab at a pass shot on his backhand side. The ball has actually passed him, yet he still is able to get his racquet on the ball.

that it doesn't come off the back wall. Learning how the ball reacts takes time, however, so don't get discouraged if your cross-court pass occasionally gives your opponent a setup. Keep trying, and one day you'll surprise both yourself and your opponent when you see that perfect cross-court pass drop in for a point.

V Pass

The V pass (Diagram 23) should be used only when you and your opponent are standing in front court at or near the center of the court. Hit the ball hard to the far left or far right of center on the front wall and

at shoulder level. On the rebound, the properly hit V pass will strike the side wall shoulder-high near the short line and bound behind your opponent, who is standing in front court.

The V pass is an especially good shot to use in doubles when both opponents are in front court. If you attempt a V pass in singles or doubles when the opposition is in back court, you'll be hitting the ball right to the receiver.

Pass shots are most effective when struck firmly with a great deal of force. If you find yourself facing an opponent who continually "blasts" the ball, be patient and stay in back court. Hopefully, your opponent soon will tire his playing arm and slacken off. Also, a hard-hitting player gives his opponent plenty of setups off the back wall.

In any case, don't try to match your opponent's hard hits, especially if you aren't naturally a power hitter. The player who concentrates on his speed and playing skills, not just sheer muscle power, will be most successful in defeating his opponent.

THE CEILING BALL . . . is the shot that changed racquetball. The game is different now, giving a control player an even chance against a shooter. Charlie Brumfield is about to hit a ceiling shot to Steve Serot's backhand, thereby forcing Steve into deep court.

chapter 5
DEFENSIVE SHOTS

The job of the defensive player is to stop his opponent from scoring. In racquetball, as in other sports, the best way to do this is by learning and mastering the basic shots of the game.

Control of front court is essential for a good defensive racquetball player. You can move forward to cover kill attempts, to either side to get pass shots, and back for balls off the back wall. If your opponent is occupying front court, you want to remove him and make him take his shots from back court.

The basic defensive shots—*ceiling ball, lob ball, Z ball,* and *around-the-wall ball*—are used to get your opponent out of front court. If properly executed, defensive shots will prevent your opponent from making his kill shots from front court.

CEILING BALL

The use of the ceiling ball (Diagram 24) has increased considerably with the manufacture of more uniform and more live balls.

Some of the top players in racquetball today use it to get themselves out of trouble during a volley.

The forehand ceiling ball is hit most often with the overhand stroke, head-high, and about 1 foot in front of the player's body. The ball must be hit firmly and high onto the ceiling, about 2-5 feet in front of the front wall. It then will come off the ceiling, angle down to hit the floor back of the short line, and bounce up and back to the back corner of the court.

If the ceiling ball is hit with the backhand stroke, the ball should be hit shoulder-high (not head-high), and the arm should be extended about 1 foot from the body at the point of contact with the ball.

The ceiling ball must be *undercut*—hit with the racquet head angled slightly down toward the floor (closed)—or it won't spin correctly. To understand how the ceiling ball spin works, take the ball or any round object and hold it between your thumb and index finger in your right hand. Rotate the

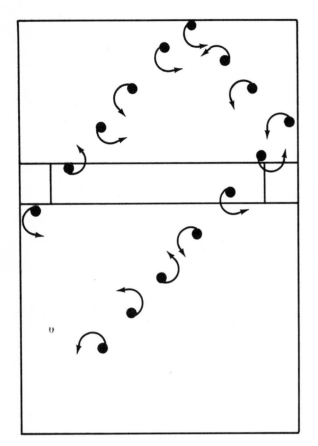

DIAGRAM 24. Bottom spin of the ceiling ball.

DIAGRAM 25. The ceiling ball (front wall first).

ball to the left (counterclockwise). This motion is called *bottom spin*, and it results when you undercut the ball. Now rotate the ball to the right (clockwise). This motion is called *top spin*, and it results from the ball's hitting the ceiling and the front wall. Reverse, or top spin, makes the ball travel farther into back court after it hits the floor.

The good ceiling ball must be hit with the proper undercutting motion and the correct amount of power, and it must strike the ceiling 2-5 feet from the front wall. Also, the player should strive to make his ceiling ball a wallpaper ball—a ball that hugs the side wall as it travels down toward the short line and hits the floor.

Most beginning racquetball players hit the ceiling ball too hard. This is a natural mistake because a player wants the ball to

travel a long distance—starting from back court and returning to deep court. Yet the ceiling ball shouldn't be hit as hard as possible because there is no direct relationship between the force of the hit and the distance the ball travels to the back wall. Also, hitting the ball as hard as possible is extremely tiring. If the ball is hit to spin properly, there is no need to blast it.

One of the most outstanding ceiling ball players today is Steve Keeley. Steve often uses the ceiling ball to rescue himself in a tough rally. "The player always should try to hit the ceiling ball 2-5 feet from the front wall," advises Keeley. "If your ball strays too far from this range, you'll have to hit it much harder to make it bounce deep to back court."

A variation of the ceiling ball is the *front-wall-first ceiling ball* (Diagram 25).

THE UNDERCUTTING MOTION . . . and the proper amount of power are the most important elements of the ceiling ball. In the pictures on this page Steve Keeley, one of the best ceiling ball players around, executes the forehand ceiling ball. Note the cocked arm in the ready position and the follow-through across the body. When you try a ceiling ball, remember not to hit the ball too hard.

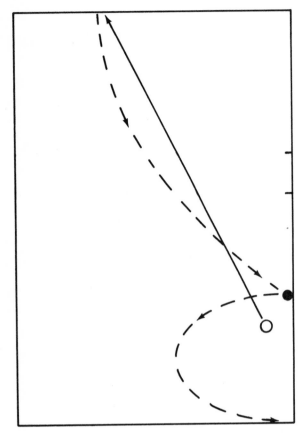

DIAGRAM 26. The lob ball.

The player stands in front court and hits the ball with almost an underhand stroke. The ball should be hit to a point high on the front wall. The momentum of the ball will make it angle upward, hit the ceiling, and rebound to the floor near the short line.

The front-wall-first ceiling ball should be hit from front court only. If hit from back court, the top spin, resulting from the ball's impact with the ceiling, won't allow the ball to carry deep enough into back court, and it will be a very easy setup for your opponent.

A properly executed ceiling ball will make your opponent rush to get into deep court for the return. If your opponent does manage to return your ceiling shot, his return most likely will be another ceiling ball. It usually will not be a kill shot.

Since a ceiling ball is easier to stroke than a hard-hit kill shot, you've nothing to lose by trying a ceiling ball when the opportunity presents itself.

Give yourself plenty of practice hours to learn the defensive ceiling ball. Concentrate especially on the amount of power you use to hit the ball. If you hit the ceiling ball too hard, it may come off the back wall instead of dropping into deep court. If you hit the ball too softly or strike the side wall near the short line, the ball will not carry deep enough and may provide your opponent with a mid-court setup.

LOB BALL

The lob (Diagram 26), when properly hit, is a tough shot for most opponents to handle. Like the offensive drop shot, the lob has become less popular among many players because of the improved ball, which has made the lob more difficult to control. Players who formerly used the lob extensively are now using ceiling balls. Even champion Charlie Brumfield admits, "I use the lob only if I can't hit anything else."

In the defensive lob shot the player must use his basic forehand or backhand stroke to hit the ball softly and firmly. The ball should be struck at a point just off the foot that is closest to the front wall and at the *apex* (highest point) of its bounce, just before it begins to drop to the floor. The greater the height at which you hit the lob, the softer you will have to hit the ball to get it to hit high on the front wall.

A properly executed lob ball will angle toward the side wall and die in deep back court. If your lob attempts consistently hit the back wall and give your opponent a set-up, you are stroking the ball too hard. Use a light, short, and firm stroke, not a long, lazy swing or jab.

Many top racquetball players hit the lob with the face of the racquet slightly open. These players feel that the slightly

THE IDEAL LOB SHOT . . . can be very difficult for opponents to return. Brumfield shows the proper way to stroke the lob. (Most players would frown on the pigeon-toed follow-through, however.)

upward angle of the racquet face helps control the ball by *taking a little off*—slowing the ball down—and insuring that the ball will drop softly into back court.

When learning the defensive lob shot, many players find it helpful to review the footwork used in the basic forehand and backhand strokes. Just because the lob shot requires that you "baby" your full hitting power slightly, this doesn't mean that you should "baby" your footwork.

Brumfield uses the lob as a change of pace shot. "Most advanced racquetball is played at a slam-bang rate of speed," says Charlie. "If in a fast, tense game you can manage to hit a high, soft lob at your opponent, he may be so surprised that he will rush his shot and hit an ineffective return."

Charlie adds: "I use the lob to force my opponent to make a shot. Hitting a slow

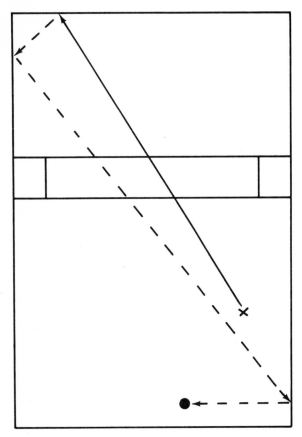

DIAGRAM 27. The forehand Z ball.

lob gives me more time to get in a good position to cover my opponent's return. And, because I'm in an ideal place, the pressure is really on my opponent to hit a good shot and not make any errors."

Z BALL

The Z ball (Diagram 27) is one of the most difficult shots to hit and to return in racquetball. It is one of the newest shots in the game and, if mastered, will give your opponent fits on the court.

You can shoot the Z ball from almost any point on the court (as long as you are standing off-center), hitting the ball with great power and firmness into the opposite corner of the front wall and letting your stroking arm follow through fully across your midsection. The ball should angle sharply to the side wall and rebound deep

to the opposite side wall in back court. The last wall that the ball hits reverses its spin so that it rebounds in a direction parallel to the back wall, making it a back wall wallpaper ball.

Your opponent will find it extremely difficult to return a Z ball. First, he must get into deep court quickly if he is to have any chance of a return. Even if he gets there in time, he will find it nearly impossible to get his racquet face squarely into the ball for a solid return. If he does make a return, it probably will be a ceiling return and not a kill. Second, your opponent probably will try to hit a Z ball out of the air from a mid-court position before it can reach the last wall. Because a properly hit Z ball travels high in the air as it zooms cross-court, your opponent will be forced to hit the ball out of the air in an awkward overhand manner that may result in a weak return.

In the 1972 International Singles Championship match between Charlie Brumfield and Ron Rubenstein, Brumfield used the Z ball extensively, forcing Rubenstein to deep court, where he was rushed into making weak returns. "He drove me crazy with those Z balls," said Rubenstein. "There was absolutely nothing I could do with them. The Z ball got me off balance and in deep court, and all I could do was flick the ball to the front wall."

AROUND-THE-WALL BALL

The around-the-wall ball is hit from deep court to the opposite side wall and then to the front wall and should rebound into the deep cross-court corner. The around-the-wall ball should not be hit as hard as the Z ball.

This effective defensive ball will move your opponent out of center court. The around-the-wall ball usually doesn't react as wildly as the Z ball because it hits two,

A PERFECT DEMONSTRATION . . . of the backhand Z ball. Keeley demonstrates proper form every step of the way: the open stance, weight transfer, open racquet face, and across-the-body follow-through. The Z ball is a tough shot, but if you can do it well, you can devastate your opponent.

STEVE KEELEY DEMONSTRATES . . . the forehand around-the-wall ball. The around-the-wall ball is not easy to master, and your opponent may be able to return it easily by taking it out of the air. You may not use this shot very often, but in order to be a well-rounded player you should be able to execute all offensive and defensive shots.

not three, walls. Also, the around-the-wall ball will not travel as high as the Z ball when it bounds cross-court, so your opponent may be able to take the ball out of the air more easily. "Also," adds Brumfield, "The around-the-wall ball is a tough shot to hit deep enough and still keep off the back wall."

A good racquetball player knows both his offensive and defensive shots. Simply being a *roadrunner*—a player who prolongs a volley by using only defensive shots and who causes his opponent to run a lot —will not make you a top-notch or well-rounded player. You may be a satisfactory player, but you'll never be an outstanding player—one who uses offensive and defensive shots with equal ability.

TIME OUT! When things aren't going right, the thing to do is call a time-out and figure out the solution. Time-outs are not necessarily used to prevent fatigue; in fact, top tournament players use time-outs more often for planning strategy than for saving energy. Here Steve Serot and Biron Valier talk over a serious situation during the 1972 international championships.

chapter 6
MIND AND BODY

Once a player has developed a mastery of racquetball skills, he should work on learning to think clearly under pressure and on keeping his body in good physical condition. A player can have a thorough understanding of the rules and a completely stocked arsenal of all the shots yet be unable to play the game skillfully if his body does not respond when it should. Also, a player will find it difficult to win any games without the proper mental attitude and correct strategy.

MENTAL ATTITUDE

Many books have been written about a player's "desire to win," a quality that, if present, separates the "good" player from the "outstanding" player. Though there are various definitions of desire, it is generally agreed that a player's mental attitude about himself and the game plays a large part in determining if he will go out there on the court and play to win or if he will hand the game to his opponent.

The effect that a player's mental attitude can have on the outcome of a game often is demonstrated in tournament play, when two players of equal or near-equal ability play each other. Time and again, the player who comes out on top is the player who keeps his confidence in his ability to win.

There are two theories about the proper way to prepare yourself mentally, to get psyched up, for a game. The first says concentrate on practicing, and then play the way you practice. The second says use the pressure of the game itself, and make it work to your advantage. Neither viewpoint is "more correct," and most players probably get mentally prepared both in their practice sessions and during the game.

Playing the way you practice is an idea that Vince Lombardi used to use when coaching his Green Bay Packers. The players practiced long and hard on football fundamentals and gradually convinced themselves that they could outexecute and outlast any team they played.

EVEN THE TOP PLAYERS . . . make mistakes. Here Steve Keeley demonstrates the "don'ts": close your eyes, tangle your feet, swing, and miss.

To play good racquetball, you also must practice long and hard so you know in your mind that you have a better mastery of the skills of the game than your opponent does. Knowing you're good, and believing it, will lead you to victory.

Some players hold themselves back during the beginning games of a tournament; they let the pressure of the game bring them to the peak of their playing ability. By the middle of the tournament, these players really begin to play to the best of their ability, often hitting what they thought were "impossible" shots in earlier matches.

Yet sometimes players who usually are quite at ease about their ability to perform will become tense and nervous before a game. If this happens to you, remember that a little nervousness—or pregame tension—actually can improve your performance on the court if you control it. A mildly nervous state will prepare your muscles to react quickly and keep your mind active and busy with thoughts about how you can counter your opponent's strengths. If you feel your nervousness getting out of hand, begin to think of all the hours you've put in practicing and preparing. On the other hand, if you begin the game completely relaxed and with no feelings of tension, the game may be over and lost before you wake up!

Above all, never worry about losing a game. This kind of negative thinking will undermine your confidence and simply give you something else to think about. When you're out there shooting on the court, you've got enough to think about. If you play your best, you'll have nothing to be sorry about—win or lose.

STRATEGY

The game of racquetball is won by the player who has *center-court control*. By dominating mid-court, a player can keep his opponent moving deep left and deep right for the returns. Also, the player who controls center court can hit the ball to the front wall from a distance of only about 20 feet (mid-court), a shot that doesn't take as much power or require as much accuracy as a shot hit from almost 40 feet (back court).

Yet while center court is the ideal position for the offensive player, the defensive player ideally tries to cover the court, working constantly to move his opponent out of the center position.

Another part of strategy relates to the fact that all players have certain playing habits, favorite shots, and patterns of executing these shots. If you can learn to anticipate your opponent's shot before he hits it, you'll have an advantage that will help you cover and return the ball.

BASIC STRATEGY . . . includes choosing the best shot. Here Ken Wong has a back-wall set up against fellow Missourian Jerry Hilecher. Wong has three options: kill in the left front corner, pass down the line, or pass cross court. What would you do?

For example, if you know that in a certain situation your opponent usually attempts a cross-court pass, you should move into back court quickly before the pass goes by you. As the defensive player, you're primarily concerned with being in the best position to retrieve the ball.

The skilled racquetball player always tries to hit a shot that he feels his opponent can't retrieve. Thus, he hits a series of shots, with each shot calculated to move his opponent slightly more out of position to retrieve the final shot that will win the volley.

"If I'm having any success in controlling the rally," says Charlie Brumfield, "I know exactly where my opponent is. And if I can get him retrieving in the back left or back right corners of the court, I know he can't recover quickly enough to regain center-court position before I hit my next shot. Then it's just a matter of hitting the ball to the side of the court opposite from where he's standing."

Many beginning racquetball players attempt to retrieve *every* ball their opponent hits. These players run about the court, constantly changing their position, and eventually tire themselves out so they no longer can play their best. Keep in mind that total coverage of the court is the ideal defensive technique and that most players don't achieve it, even by using the technique of anticipation.

"If my opponent hits a shot from the right side of the court, down the line, and one inch high," says Brumfield, "I can't cover it from back court. So I don't even *pretend* I can. I spend my time concentrating on the areas that I know will give me my strongest returns."

If you get into a losing streak during a game and your opponent has you off-balance, running all over the court, go for a few winners—kill shots. If you can manage to kill the ball successfully a few times, you'll feel more confident and give your opponent something to worry about. Unless you take the offensive, your opponent will keep the ball in play until you tire or make a mistake that will give him the point.

Don't forget that your opponent has his own game-winning strategy in mind. Any time you can force him to counter your kills with some difficult shooting of his own, you'll put him on the defensive and make him change his overall game plan. Show your opponent that you can move him about on the court, and show him that you're alert and ready to return any shot he can hit.

There are usually turning points in a game—certain rallies that, if won, will give one player a safe margin of points over his opponent. The player who grabs the lead can hit a bit more freely, and the player who trails in points is forced to play error-less racquetball. Show yourself and your opponent that you aren't the kind of player who chokes up at the crucial points of the game.

Doubles

In doubles play each player is one-half of a team, and neither player can win the game or match without the other. Playing doubles will help sharpen one's singles playing ability because a player must hit more accurately in doubles. Frequent *corner shots* and V passes keep each player on his toes. While the shots are the same both in singles and doubles, the presence of four players on the court creates an entirely different playing situation, which must be taken into account in deciding how points can be made and how the opposing team's shots can best be covered.

Before the game each team should decide the responsibilities each partner will have in covering the court. There are three primary methods of court coverage in doubles: *half-and-half, three-quarters one-quarter,* and *I-formation.*

Half-and-half is the most common method of playing doubles. Each partner is responsible for one side of the court; that is, the backhand side player covers the left court, and the forehand side player covers the right court. The players may trade areas temporarily when one player is out of position and unable to cover his territory.

On their way to the 1972 International Doubles Championship, Mike Luciw and George Rudysz played half-and-half style racquetball. They always tried to keep themselves separated by an invisible line down the court, and neither of them often strayed beyond that line.

In three-quarters one-quarter court coverage each player has responsibility for an area marked off by an invisible line drawn from one front corner to the opposite back court corner.

The three-quarter one-quarter method enables a team with a particularly outstanding back wall shooter to cover all shots that come off the back wall or a quick retrieving player to cover most of the short shots.

A DOUBLES LESSON. Establish a clear communications system with your partner. In doubles you are only half of a team, and neither of you can win without the other. Communications apparently broke down here, as two partners, Roger Souders and Dave Charlson, attempted to strike the ball at the same time.

The third method of playing doubles is the I-formation—one partner in front court and one in deep court. The front court partner usually will not have to play as strenuously as the back court partner.

When you use the I-formation, it is best to place a less-conditioned player in front court because he will tire less easily as the game progresses.

The back court partner in I-formation doubles is often an outstanding ceiling ball or deep court shooter. However, if the deep court partner misses a kill shot, for example,

his partner in front court must be fast enough to cover any re-kill attempts.

A good doubles team always tries to dominate center court. From this position, players can kill or pass; defensively, they can move back for back wall shots or cover kill attempts made by their opponents.

Doubles players often use an isolation strategy in their game, whereby neither partner hits the ball to the opponent who is having a hot streak, that is, hitting a successful series of shots. In isolation strategy, virtually every ball is hit to the

FAST-ACTION PLAY . . . can make for a crowded court. Here Craig Finger extends for a shot in doubles play. Bill Schmidtke moves out of the way to allow Craig an unobstructed shot. Failure to do so would result in an avoidable hinder, and the point would be awarded to Finger's team.

partner of the "hot" player, thus isolating the better player from the volley. When you or your partner think the better player is convinced that you're not going to hit the ball to him, hit a hard drive shot at him. He often will be so surprised by this move that your side will pick up an easy point.

Another strategy that works well both in singles and doubles is to exploit your opponents' weak areas. If one opponent's backhand is weak, keep hitting him backhand shots. Or if you notice an opponent is not shooting particularly well, get in there and cut off his pass shots, leaving him no choice but to use a shot that doesn't seem to be working.

Good doubles strategy involves working closely with your partner. Set up a method of communication so you will know who takes a shot if both of you have a chance at it. If your partner gets caught up front, in deep court, or anywhere out of position, cover defense for him or, on the offense, hit a lob or ceiling ball to give him more time to regain his position.

Keep your eyes on the ball no matter who is hitting it. If your partner should swing and miss the ball, you might be able to retrieve it. If you're looking elsewhere, you may miss such an opportunity.

PHYSICAL CONDITIONING

A good way to insure that you'll be able to

control the play in a game is to make sure that your body is in excellent physical condition. Your opponent hardly will feel challenged if he sees you dragging about the court and consistently hitting weak returns after only a few volleys.

Practicing good eating habits will help you get in top condition. Make sure you eat balanced meals and don't fill up on junk foods between meals. Remember that foods high in sugar or starch tend to add weight that will slow you down on the court.

Eat sensible meals that combine lean meat, fresh fruit, and vegetables. Avoid greasy or fried foods; they will give you a queasy stomach when you're out on the court.

Top players always try to get enough sleep. Eight hours of sleep a night is considered an average amount for most people, but the amount varies for each individual. Of course, you'll probably want to get a bit more sleep the night before you have a particularly strenuous workout or several games in a row.

In racquetball, as in any sport, the best players are the ones who train the hardest. Because these players are devoted to the game, they willingly and consciously make the sacrifice of using their spare time to get and stay in shape.

Perhaps the toughest obstacle a racquetball player faces is fatigue—the point at which the body no longer responds to what the mind tells it to do. Needless to say, when you become fatigued in a game, you're in a dangerous situation, for no matter how well you can play, your body will continue to respond slowly and ineffectively.

Improving your knowledge of game strategy and your playing skills are two ways to reduce the factor of fatigue. Another way is to condition your body to withstand tremendous physical demands.

Running and jogging (slower-paced but constant running) are excellent ways to get in shape. This kind of exercise strengthens and firms your leg muscles, expands your lung capacity, and improves your blood circulation.

Many champion players begin their conditioning one month before a big tournament, jogging one or two miles daily to start. By the second week, a player begins to "push" himself, increasing his running distance and speed but being careful not to overextend himself. The final two weeks before the tournament are spent doing *buildups*—jogging steadily for 1/8 mile, sprinting 1/8 mile, jogging 1/8 mile, and so forth. While most tournament players readily admit that doing buildups is not much fun, they are quick to point out that they are essential if a player wants to avoid becoming exhausted early in the game.

Continuous practice is another way to get in shape. Paul Haber, five-time winner of the U.S. Handball Singles Championship, gets in shape for national tournaments by playing handball 5-6 hours daily or until he barely can lift his arms.

Very few racquetball players can practice as long as Paul practices his handball before tournaments, especially since racquetball courts are in high demand and oftentimes are shared with handball players.

A good rule of thumb is to work out as often and long as you can. Remember, though, that simply practicing one hour a day a few times each week will not provide enough of a workout to reduce the factor of game fatigue.

Use your practice sessions wisely, concentrating on your footwork and proper stroking motions, practicing more difficult shots, and improving your overall playing form.

While practicing alone is a good way to

THE 1972 NATIONAL INVITATIONAL DOUBLES finals. The NID tourney is one of the major events of the year, and to prepare for the competition these players have practiced hard and tuned up in as many preliminary tournaments as possible.

improve your playing skills, only by playing with others will you be able to assess your playing ability realistically and profit from the desire to improve that competition creates.

Many players find it helpful to play in small regional tournaments. Although there is not yet a racquetball "tour"—prearranged competition in various cities—as there is in tennis and golf, there are many independent tournaments that take place throughout the country. Listings of these smaller, approved tournaments are listed in *Racquetball* magazine. Even if you don't feel you're up to competing in these tournaments right

now, you still can attend these competitions and profit from watching more skilled players compete.

Champion players use these smaller "tune-up" tournaments to check up on their general physical condition and to determine whether their playing has any weak spots. With the knowledge gained from these competitions, players can increase their build-ups or practice sessions to patch up any weak spots before they become difficult-to-break habits.

"If you have time only to run or to play racquetball but not to do both," says Steve Keeley, 1971 National Champion, "then by all means play. But without running to keep in shape, you'll never have the power that will win you crucial matches."

The combination of a properly conditioned body and a good mental attitude will be rewarded by the satisfaction you'll feel after winning a game. Then, too, if you're playing fundamentally correct racquetball—keeping your eyes on the ball, using the proper strokes, and choosing the right shot for a given situation—you'll be well on your way to becoming a champion competitor. You may not win all the volleys or every game you play, but you'll be a consistently good player, and you'll strike fear in the heart of your opponent.

RACQUETBALL IS A GAME FOR EVERYONE. In a Masters doubles match both men on a team must be 40 years old, and one of them has to be at least 45. Thus the Masters have a chance to continue competition on a national level and are not forced to give away precious years to much younger opponents.

chapter 7
IRA RULES

The International Racquetball Association was formed in 1968 through the resources and leadership of the U.S. Handball Association. A nonprofit service organization, the IRA is dedicated to promoting the physical and mental well-being of people of all nations through the sport of racquetball. Today, over 3,000 persons are members of the IRA.

The Association has many functions, including publishing and keeping up-to-date the official rules of the game and sponsoring and approving hundreds of tournaments. Only IRA members may compete in officially sanctioned tournaments.

The IRA is supported by contributions from its members and by a small percentage of the income derived from players' purchases of products bearing the official seal of the Association.

Headquarters for the Association are at 4101 Dempster Street, Skokie, Illinois 60076. The headquarters serves as a clearinghouse for all information pertaining to racquetball.

The following are the official IRA four-wall rules for racquetball.

1. The Game

Rule 1.1—Types of Games. Racquetball may be played by two or four players. When played by two it is called "singles," and when played by four, "doubles."

Rule 1.2—Description. Racquetball, as the name implies, is a competitive game in which a racquet is used to serve and return the ball.

Rule 1.3—Objective. The objective is to win each volley by serving or returning the ball so the opponent is unable to keep the ball in play. A serve or volley is won when a side is unable to return the ball before it touches the floor twice.

Rule 1.4—Points and Outs. Points are scored only by the serving side when it serves an ace or wins a volley. When the serving side loses a volley, it loses the serve. Losing the serve is called an "out" in singles, and a "hand-out" in doubles.

Rule 1.5—Game. A game is won by the side first scoring 21 points.

Rule 1.6—Match. A match is won by the side first winning two games.

2. Courts and Equipment

Rule 2.1—Courts. The specifications for the standard four-wall racquetball court are:

(a) **Dimension.** The dimensions shall be 20 feet wide, 20 feet high, and 40 feet long, with back wall at least 12 feet high.

(b) **Lines and Zones.** All racquetball courts shall be divided and marked on the floors with 1½ inch wide red or white lines as follows:

(1) **Short Line.** The short line is midway between and is parallel with the front and back walls dividing the court into equal front and back courts.

(2) **Service Line.** The service line is parallel with and located 5 feet in front of the short line.

(3) **Service Zone.** The service zone is the space between the outer edges of the short and service lines.

(4) **Service Boxes.** A service box is located at each end of the service zone by lines 18 inches from and parallel to each side wall.

(5) **Receiving Lines.** Five feet back of the short line, vertical lines shall be marked on each side wall extending 3 inches from the floor. See rule 4.7(a).

Rule 2.2—Ball Specifications. The speci-

fications for the standard racquetball are:

(a) **Official Ball.** IRA's official ball is the black Seamless 558. The ball shall be 2¼ inches in diameter, weigh approximately 1.40 ounces, and have a bounce at 65-70 inches from 100 inch drop at a temperature of 76 degrees F.

Rule 2.3—Ball Selection. A new ball shall be selected by the referee for use in each match in all tournaments. During a game the referee may, at his discretion or at the request of both players or teams, select another ball. Balls that are not round or which bounce erratically shall not be used. The Seamless 558 ball is official for all IRA sanctioned tournaments.

Rule 2.4—Racquet Specifications. The specifications for the standard racquetball racquet are:

(a) **Official Racquet.** IRA's official racquets are the Sportcraft 13178 and 13188 (wood frames), 13175 (aluminum frame), and 13185 (steel frame).

(b) **Dimensions.** The official racquet will have a maximum head length of 11 inches and a width of 9 inches. These measurements are computed from the outer edge of the racquet head rims. The handle may not exceed 7 inches in length. Total length and width of the racquet may not exceed a total of 27 inches.

(c) **Thong.** The racquet must include a thong that must be securely wrapped on the player's wrist.

(d) **Frame.** The racquet frame may be made of any material, as long as it conforms to the above specifications.

(e) **Strings.** The strings of the racquet must be gut, monofilament, or nylon but cannot be of steel or metal.

Rule 2.5—Uniform. All parts of the uniform, consisting of a shirt, shorts, socks, and shoes, shall be clean and light or bright in color. Warmup shirts and pants, if worn in actual match play, shall also be white, light, or bright but may be of any color if not used in actual match play. In IRA-sanctioned tournaments, the tournament chairman or his delegated representative shall instruct doubles teams to wear uniforms of a different color. Only club insignia and/or name of club or racquetball organization may be on the uniform. Players may not play without shirts.

3. Officiating

Rule 3.1—Tournaments. All tournaments shall be managed by a committee or chairman, who shall designate the officials.

Rule 3.2—Officials. The officials shall include a referee and a scorer. Additional assistants and record keepers may be designated as desired.

Rule 3.3—Qualifications. Since the quality of the officiating often determines the success of each tournament, all officials shall be experienced or trained and shall be thoroughly familiar with these rules and with the local playing conditions.

Rule 3.4—Briefing. Before all tournaments, all officials and players shall be briefed on rules and on local court hinders or other regulations.

Rule 3.5—Referees.

(a) **Pre-Match Duties.** Before each match commences, it shall be the duty of the referee to:

(1) Check on adequacy of preparation of the court with respect to cleanliness, lighting, and temperature, and upon location of locker rooms, drinking fountains, etc.

(2) Check on availability and suitability of all materials necessary for the match such as balls, towels, score cards, and pencils.

(3) Check readiness and qualifications of assisting officials.

(4) Explain court regulations to players and inspect the compliance of racquets with rules.

(5) Remind players to have an extra supply of adequate racquets and uniforms.

(6) Introduce players, toss coin, and signal start of first game.

(b) **Decisions.** During games the referee shall decide all questions that may arise in accordance with these rules. If there is body contact on the backswing, the player should call it quickly. This is the only call a player may make. On all questions involving judgment and on all questions not covered by these rules, the decision of the referee is final.

(c) **Protests.** Any decision not involving the judgment of the referee may on protest be decided by the chairman, if present, or his delegated representative.

(d) **Forfeitures.** A match may be forfeited by the referee when:

(1) Any player refuses to abide by the referee's decision or engages in unsportsmanlike conduct.

(2) After warning, any player leaves the court without permission of the referee either during a game or between the first and second games.

(3) Any player for a singles match or any team for a doubles match fails to report to play. Normally, 20 minutes from the scheduled game time will be allowed before forfeiture. The tournament chairman may permit a longer delay if circumstances warrant such a decision.

(4) If both players for a singles or both teams for doubles fail to appear to play for consolation matches or other play-

offs, they shall forfeit their ratings for future tournaments, and forfeit any trophies, medals, or awards.

Rule 3.6—Scorers. The scorer shall keep a record of the progress of the game in the manner prescribed by the committee or chairman. As a minimum the progress record shall include the order of serves, outs, and points. The referee or scorer shall announce the score before each serve.

Rule 3.7—Record Keepers. In addition to the scorer, the committee may designate additional persons to keep more detailed records for statistical purposes of the progress of the game.

4. Play Regulations

Rule 4.1—Serve (Generally).

(a) **Order.** The player or side winning the toss becomes the first server and starts the first game and the third game, if any.

(b) **Start.** Games are started by the referee calling, "Play ball."

(c) **Place.** The server may serve from any place in the service zone. No part of either foot may extend beyond either line of the service zone. Stepping on the line (but not beyond it) is permitted. Server must remain in the service zone until the served ball passes short line. Violations are called "foot faults."

(d) **Manner.** A serve is commenced by bouncing the ball to the floor in the service zone, and on the first bounce the ball is struck by the server's racquet so that it hits the front wall and on the rebound hits the floor back of the short line, either with or without touching one of the side walls.

(e) **Readiness.** Serves shall not be made until the receiving side is ready, or the referee has called, "Play ball."

Rule 4.2—Serve (In Doubles).

(a) **Server.** At the beginning of each game in doubles, each side shall inform the referee of the order of service, which order shall be followed throughout the game. Only the first server serves the first time up and continues to serve first throughout the game. When the first server is out—the side is out. Thereafter both players on each side shall serve until a hand-out occurs. It is not necessary for the server to alternate serves to their opponents.

(b) **Partner's Position.** On each serve, the server's partner shall stand erect with his back to the side wall and with both feet on the floor within the service box until the served ball passes the short line. Violations are called "foot faults."

Rule 4.3—Defective Serves. Defective serves are of three types, resulting in penalties as follows:

(a) **Dead Ball Serve.** A dead ball serve results in no penalty and the server is given another serve without canceling a prior illegal serve.

(b) **Fault Serve.** Two fault serves result in a hand-out.

(c) **Out Serves.** An out serve results in a hand-out.

Rule 4.4—Dead Ball Serves. Dead ball serves do not cancel any previous illegal serve. They occur when an otherwise legal serve:

(a) **Hits Partner.** Hits the server's partner on the fly on the rebound from the front wall while the server's partner is in the service box. Any serve that touches the floor before hitting the partner in the box is a short.

(b) **Screen Balls.** Passes too close to the server or the server's partner to obstruct the view of the returning side. Any serve passing behind the server's partner and the side wall is an automatic screen.

(c) **Court Hinders.** Hits any part of the court that under local rules is a dead ball.

Rule 4.5—Fault Serves. The following serves are faults, and any two in succession results in a hand-out:

(a) **Foot Faults.** A foot fault results:

(1) When the server leaves the service zone before the served ball passes the short line.

(2) When the server's partner leaves the service zone before the served ball passes the short line.

(b) **Short Serve.** A short serve is any served ball that first hits the front wall and on the rebound hits the floor in front of the back edge of the short line either with or without touching one side wall.

(c) **Three-Wall Serve.** A two-side serve is any ball served that first hits the front wall and on the rebound hits two side walls on the fly.

(d) **Ceiling Serve.** A ceiling serve is any served ball that touches the ceiling after hitting the front wall either with or without touching one side wall.

(e) **Long Serve.** A long serve is any served ball that first hits the front wall and rebounds to the back wall before touching the floor.

(f) **Out of Court Serve.** Any ball going out of the court on the serve.

Rule 4.6—Out Serves. Any one of the following serves results in a hand-out:

(a) **Bounces.** Bouncing the ball more than three times while in the service zone before striking the ball. One bounce is counted each time the ball hits the floor within the service zone. Once the server is within the service zone and the receiver is ready, the ball may not be bounced anywhere but on the floor within the service zone. Accidental dropping of the ball counts as one bounce.

(b) **Missed Ball.** Any attempt to strike the ball on the first bounce that results either in a total miss or in touching any part of the server's body other than his racquet.

(c) **Nonfront Serve.** Any served ball that strikes the server's partner, or the ceiling, floor, or side wall, before striking the front wall.

(d) **Touched Serve.** Any served ball that on the rebound from the front wall touches the server, or touches the server's partner while any part of his body is out of the service box, or the server's partner intentionally catches the served ball on the fly.

(e) **Out-of-Order Serve.** In doubles, when either partner serves out of order. Any points which may have been scored during an out-of-order serve will be automatically void with the score reverting to the score prior to the out-of-order serve.

(f) **Crotch Serve.** If the served ball hits the crotch in the front wall, it is considered the same as hitting the floor and is an out. A crotch serve into the back wall is good and in play.

Rule 4.7—Return of Serve.

(a) **Receiving Position.** The receiver or receivers must stand at least 5 feet back of the short line, as indicated by the 3-inch vertical line on each side wall, and cannot return the ball until it passes the short line. Any infraction results in a point for the server.

(b) **Defective Serve.** To eliminate any misunderstanding the receiving side should not catch or touch a defectively served ball until called by the referee or it has touched the floor for the second time.

(c) **Fly Return.** In making a fly return, no part of the receiver's body or racquet may enter into the service zone. A violation by a receiver results in a point for the server.

(d) Legal Return. After the ball is legally served, one of the players on the receiving side must strike the ball with his racquet either on the fly or after the first bounce and before the ball touches the floor the second time to return the ball to the front wall either directly or after touching one or both side walls, the back wall, or the ceiling, or any combination of those surfaces. A returned ball may not touch the floor before touching the front wall. (It is legal to return the ball by striking the ball into the back wall first, then hitting the front wall on the fly or after hitting the side wall or ceiling.)

(e) Failure to Return. The failure to return a serve results in a point for the server.

Rule 4.8—Changes of Serve.

(a) Hand-out. A server is entitled to continue serving until:

(1) Out Serve. He makes an out serve under Rule 4.6.

(2) Fault Serves. He makes two fault serves in succession under Rule 4.5.

(3) Hits Partner. He hits his partner with an attempted return before the ball touches the floor a second time.

(4) Return Failure. He or his partner fails to keep the ball in play by returning it as required by Rule 4.7(d).

(5) Avoidable Hinder. He or his partner commits an avoidable hinder under Rule 4.11.

(b) Side-out.

(1) In Singles. In singles, retiring the server retires the side.

(2) In Doubles. In doubles, the side is retired when both partners have been put out, except on the first serve as provided in Rule 4.2(a).

(c) Effect. When the server or the side

loses the serve, the server or serving side shall become the receiver; and the receiving side, the server; and so alternately in all subsequent services of the game.

Rule 4.9—Volleys. Each legal return after the serve is called a volley. Play during volleys shall be according to the following rules:

(a) One or Both Hands. Only the head of the racquet may be used at any time to return the ball. The ball must be hit with the racquet in one or both hands. Switching hands to hit a ball is an out. The use of any portion of the body is an out.

(b) One Touch. In attempting returns, the ball may be touched only once by one player on the returning side. In doubles both partners may swing at but only one may hit the ball. Each violation of (a) or (b) results in a hand-out or point.

(c) Return Attempts.

(1) In Singles. In singles, if a player swings at but misses the ball in play, the player may repeat his attempt to return the ball until it touches the floor the second time.

(2) In Doubles. In doubles if one player swings at but misses the ball, both he and his partner may make further attempts to return the ball until it touches the floor the second time. Both partners on a side are entitled to an attempt to return the ball.

(3) Hinders. In singles or doubles, if a player swings at but misses the ball in play, and in his or his partner's attempt again to play the ball there is an unintentional interference by an opponent it shall be a hinder. (See Rule 4.10.)

(d) Touching Ball. Except as provided in Rule 4.10 (a) (2), any touching of a ball before it touches the floor the second time by a player other than the one making a return is a point or out against the offending player.

(e) **Out of Court Ball.**

(1) **After Return.** Any ball returned to the front wall which on the rebound or on the first bounce goes into the gallery or through any opening in a side wall shall be declared dead and the serve replayed.

(2) **No Return.** Any ball not returned to the front wall, but which caroms off a player's racquet into the gallery or into any opening in a side wall either with or without touching the ceiling, side, or back wall, shall be an out or point against the players failing to make the return.

(f) **Dry Ball.** During the game and particularly on service every effort should be made to keep the ball dry. Deliberately wetting shall result in an out. The ball may be inspected by the referee at any time during a game.

(g) **Broken Ball.** If there is any suspicion that a ball has broken on the serve or during a volley, play shall continue until the end of the volley. The referee or any player may request the ball be examined. If the referee decides the ball is broken or otherwise defective, a new ball shall be put into play and the point replayed.

(h) **Play Stoppage.**

(1) If a player loses a shoe or other equipment, or foreign objects enter the court, or any other outside interference occurs, the referee shall stop the play.

(2) If a player loses control of his racquet, time should be called after the point has been decided, providing the racquet does not strike an opponent or interfere with ensuing play.

Rule 4.10—Dead Ball Hinders. Hinders are of two types—"dead ball" and "avoidable." Dead ball hinders as described in this rule result in the point being replayed. Avoidable hinders are described in 4.11.

(a) **Situations.** When called by the referee, the following are dead ball hinders:

(1) **Court Hinders.** Hits any part of the court which under local rules is a dead ball.

(2) **Hitting Opponent.** Any returned ball that touches an opponent on the fly before it returns to the front wall.

(3) **Body Contact.** Any body contact with an opponent that interferes with seeing or returning ball.

(4) **Screen Ball.** Any ball rebounding from the front wall close to the body of a player on the side which just returned the ball, to interfere with or prevent the returning side from seeing the ball. See Rule 4.4 (b).

(5) **Straddle Ball.** A ball passing between the legs of a player on the side which just returned the ball, if there is no fair chance to see or return the ball.

(6) **Other Interference.** Any other unintentional interference which prevents an opponent from having a fair chance to see or return the ball.

(b) **Effect.** A call by the referee of a "hinder" stops the play and voids any situation following, such as the ball hitting a player. No player is authorized to call a hinder except on the backswing, and such a call must be made immediately, as indicated in Rule 3.5(b).

(c) **Avoidance.** In the process of attempting to return the ball, a player is entitled to a fair chance to see and return the ball. It is the duty of the side that has just served or returned the ball to move so that the receiving side may go straight to the ball and not be required to go around an opponent. The referee should be liberal in calling hinders to discourage any practice of playing the ball where an adversary cannot see it until too late. It is no excuse that the ball is "killed," unless in the opinion of the referee the ball could not be returned.

Hinders should be called without a claim by a player, especially in close plays and on game points.

(d) **In Doubles.** In doubles, both players on a side are entitled to a fair and unobstructed chance at the ball and either one is entitled to a hinder even though it naturally would be his partner's ball and even though his partner may have attempted to play the ball or that he may already have missed it. It is not a hinder when one player hinders his partner.

Rule 4.11—Avoidable Hinders. An avoidable hinder results in an "out" or a point, depending upon whether the offender was serving or receiving.

(a) **Failure to Move.** Does not move sufficiently to allow opponent his shot.

(b) **Blocking.** Moves into a position effecting a block on the opponent about to return the ball, or, in doubles, one partner moves in front of an opponent as his partner is returning the ball.

(c) **Moving into Ball.** Moves in the way and is struck by the ball just played by his opponent.

(d) **Pushing.** Deliberately pushing or shoving an opponent during a volley.

Rule 4.12—Rest Periods.

(a) **Delays.** Deliberate delay exceeding ten seconds by server or receiver shall result in an out or point against the offender.

(b) **During Game.** During a game each player in singles, or each side in doubles, either while serving or receiving may request a "time out" for a towel, wiping glasses, change or adjustment. Each "time out" shall not exceed 30 seconds. No more than three "time outs" in a game shall be granted each singles player or each team in doubles.

(c) **Injury.** No time out shall be charged to a player who is injured during play. An injured player shall not be allowed more than a total of 15 minutes of rest. If the injured player is not able to resume play after a total rest of 15 minutes, the match shall be awarded to the opponent or opponents. On any further injury to same player, the commissioner, if present, or committee, after considering any available medical opinion shall determine whether the injured player will be allowed to continue.

(d) **Faulty Equipment.** A time out may be called by the referee, at the request of a player and after substantiation by the referee, because of faulty equipment or uniform. Two minutes are to be allowed for any uniform adjustment needed and 30 seconds for any equipment adjustment.

(e) **Between Games.** A 2-minute rest period is allowed between the first and second games, at which time the players should *not* leave the court, without approval of the referee. A 10-minute rest period is allowed between the second and third games, at which time players may leave the court.

(f) **Postponed Games.** Any games postponed by referee due to weather elements shall be resumed with the same score as when postponed.

Rule 4.13—Masters. Forty will be minimum age for all competition in singles. In doubles, one participant must be at least 40; the second must be at least 45 years of age.

5. Tournaments

Rule 5.1—Draws.

(a) If possible, the singles draw shall be made at least two days before the tournament commences. The seeding method of drawing shall be approved by the International Racquetball Association.

(b) The draw and seeding committee shall be chaired by the IRA Executive Secretary and shall consist of the Executive Secretary, the National Executive Co-ordinator, and the host tournament chairman. No other persons shall participate in the draw or seeding unless at the invitation of the draw and seeding committee.

(c) In local, state, and divisional tournaments the draw shall be the responsibility of the tournament chairman. In divisional play the tournament chairman should work in coordination with the IRA representative at the tournament.

Rule 5.2—Scheduling.

(a) **Preliminary Matches.** If one or more contestants are entered in both singles and doubles, they may be required to play both singles and doubles on the same day or night with little rest between matches. This is a risk assumed on entering both singles and doubles. If possible, the schedule should provide at least a 1-hour rest period between all matches.

(b) **Final Matches.** Where one or more players have reached the finals in both singles and doubles, it is recommended that the doubles match be played on the day preceding the singles. This would assume more rest between the final matches. If both final matches must be played on the same day or night, the following procedure is recommended: (1) The singles match be played first. (2) A rest period of not less than *1 hour* be allowed between the finals in singles and doubles.

Rule 5.3—Notice of Matches.
After the first round of matches, it is the responsibility of each player to check the posted schedules to determine the time and place of each subsequent match. If any change is made in the schedule after posting, it shall be the duty of the committee or chairman to notify the players of the change.

Rule 5.4—Third Place.
In championship tournaments, national, state, district, etc., the loser in the semifinals must play for third place or lose his ranking for the next year unless he is unable to compete because of injury or illness. (See Rule 3.5(d)(4).)

Rule 5.5—IRA Divisional Tournaments.
Starting in 1969-70 the United States was divided into five divisions.

(a) Only players residing in the area defined can participate in a division tournament.

(b) Players can participate in only two events in a division tournament.

(c) Winners of open singles and open doubles of divisional tournaments will receive round trip air coach tickets to the IRA International Tournament. Remuneration will be made after arrival, entry, and play of at least one match.

(1) If the winner(s) of open singles or open doubles has previously won such trip through qualification in a previous IRA-sanctioned tournament, the second place finisher(s) shall be awarded such trip. If the second place finisher(s) also has won such award previously, the third place finisher(s) shall be awarded such trip, and so on.

(2) Doubles teams winning divisional championships must remain intact and compete as such in the International Tournament to qualify for this award.

(d) An IRA national officer will be in attendance at each divisional tournament and will coordinate with the host chairman.

(e) **Awards.** No individual award in IRA-sanctioned tournaments should exceed value of $25.

(f) **Tournament Management.** In all IRA-sanctioned tournaments the tournament chairman and/or the national IRA official in attendance may decide on a change of courts after the completion of any tournament game if such a change will accommodate better spectator conditions.

(g) **Tournament Conduct.** In all IRA-sanctioned tournaments the referee is empowered to default a match if an individual player or team conducts itself to the detriment of the tournament and the game.

(h) **Amateur Definition.** We hold as eligible for racquetball tournaments anyone except those who engage in or promote racquetball for a profit.

(i) **Pick-A-Partner.** The essence of the "Players' Fraternity" has been to allow players to come to tournaments and select a partner, if necessary, regardless what organization or city he might represent.

6. One-wall and Three-wall Rules

Basically, racquetball rules for one-wall, three-wall, and four-wall are the same with the following exceptions:

(a) **One-Wall—Court Size.** Wall shall be 20 feet in width and 16 feet high, floor 20 feet in width and 34 feet from the wall to the back edge of the long line. There should be a minimum of 3 feet beyond the long line and 6 feet outside each side line and behind the long line to permit movement area for the players.

(b) **One-wall—Short Line.** Back edge 16 feet from the wall. Service markers—lines at least 6 inches long parallel to and midway between the long and short lines, extending in from the side lines. The imaginary extension and joining of these lines indicates the service line. Lines are 1½ inches in width. Service zone—floor area inside and including the short, side, and service lines. Receiving zone—floor area in back of short line bounded by and including the long and side lines.

(c) **Three-wall—Serve.** A serve that goes beyond the side walls on the fly is player or side out. A serve that goes beyond the long line on a fly but within the side walls is the same as a "short."

glossary

Ace: Legal serve that eludes the receiver. One point is scored.

Apex: Highest point in a bounce.

Around-the-wall-ball: Shot that hits first the side wall, then the front wall, rebounding to the side from which it was originally struck.

Around-the-wall return: An around-the-wall ball used as a return of service.

Avoidable hinder: Avoidable interference, not necessarily intentional, by one player with another's clear shot. Penalty is loss of serve or point.

Back court: Court area behind the short line.

Backhand: Fundamental stroke hit across your body, starting on the side opposite the hand with which you play. (A right-hander's backhand stroke is from left to right across his body.)

Backhand corner: That area of the court where the side wall and back wall meet; the same side as the player's backhand.

Backhand grip: The position of the hand on the racquet when stroking the backhand.

Backswing: The first step in any stroke, consisting of bringing the racquet into a ready position.

Back wall: The rear wall.

Back wall shot: Shot made from rebound off the rear wall.

Block: A maneuver executed to prevent your opponent from viewing the ball (also called a screen).

Bottom spin: Rotation of the ball in a counterclockwise direction.

Buildups: Conditioning exercises consisting of gradual jog to sprint and back to jog.

Bumper guard: Protective covering on the rim of the racquet head.

Ceiling ball: Ball that hits first the ceiling, then the front wall (or reverse), rebounding to deep court.

Ceiling return: A ceiling ball used as a service return.

Ceiling serve: A serve that hits the ceiling after hitting the front wall. This is illegal and results in a fault.

Center court control: Maintaining position in center court, and forcing your opponent to retrieve in deep court.

Change-of-pace shot: Any shot hit softer than normal.

Club play: Informal competition at local facilities.

Control: The ability to hit the ball to an intended spot.

Corner shot: Any shot that hits at or near the front right or front left corner.

Court hinder: Interference by an obstacle that deflects ball (a light fixture, latch, etc.); point is replayed.

Cross-court drive return: A relatively hard-hit service return that hits the front wall and passes the server on the side opposite that from which the shot came.

Cross-court pass shot: A cross-court pass hit during play. *See also* cross-court serve.

Cross-court serve: A serve that hits first the front wall, then the side wall, bounding to deep court on the side opposite the wall just struck.

Crotch: A juncture of two playing surfaces.

Crotch serve: Serve that strikes the juncture of the front wall and the floor or ceiling; illegal.

Crowding: Playing too close to your opponent.

Cutthroat: Game with three players with each server during his turn playing against the other two players.

Dead ball: Any ball out of play; a racquetball that does not bounce as high as normal.

Defensive shot: A return shot usually made to continue the rally rather than to end it.

Die: A ball that barely reaches the front wall and rebounds with little or no bounce is said to die.

Dig: To retrieve a low shot before it strikes the floor twice.

Doubles: Game of two teams of two players each.

Down-the-line pass shot: A shot hit from near a side wall directly to the front wall and rebounding back along the same wall.

Drive return: A relatively hard-hit service return striking only the front wall.

Drive serve: A relatively hard-hit serve that strikes the front wall and rebounds in a straight line to deep court.

Drop shot: A soft-hit ball aimed low into the front wall from front court.

Error: Failure to return an apparently playable ball.

Exchange: *See* rally.

Fault: Illegal serve or other infraction of serving rules.

Flat roll-out: A perfect kill shot: the ball hits the front wall so close to the floor that it rebounds with no bounce.

Float: A ball that travels so slowly that your opponent has enough time to set up for his next shot.

Fly ball: Shot played on rebound from front wall before it hits floor.

Follow-through: The completion of your swing after contact with the ball.

Foot fault: Illegal placement of your foot outside the service zone during serve.

Footwork: Moving your feet in the correct relationship to the rest of your body, the ball, and the racquet.

Forehand: Fundamental stroke hit across your body from the same side as the hand with which you play. (A right-handed player's forehand stroke is from right to left across his body.

Front court: Area in front of the short line.

Front line: *See* service line.

Front-wall-first ceiling ball: A shot that strikes first the front wall, then the ceiling.

Front-wall-first ceiling return: A ceiling ball return of service that strikes first the front wall, then the ceiling, rebounding to deep court.

Front wall-side wall kill: A kill shot that hits first the front wall, then the side wall. *See also* kill.

Game: Twenty-one points.

Garfinkel serve: A forehand cross-court serve to an opponent's forehand.

Grip: The manner in which the racquet is held.

Half-and-half: Definition of court responsibilities in doubles: an imaginary line is drawn down the middle of the court.

Hand-out: Loss of serve by first partner serving for his team in doubles.

Handshake grip: Method of holding racquet in handshake manner.

Head: Hitting surface of the racquet; the face.

I formation: Definition of court responsibilities in doubles: one player plays front court, and his partner plays back court.

IRA: International Racquetball Association, the governing body of racquetball.

Inning: A complete round of play in which both sides serve.

Isolation strategy: The hitting of several consecutive shots to one player in doubles and very few to his partner.

Kill: Shot that hits the front wall and rebounds too close to the floor to be returned.

Live ball: Any ball in play: a racquetball with a high bounce.

Lob ball: A soft-hit shot.

Lob return: A high, soft return of serve.

Lob serve: A high, soft service.

Long serve: Any serve that rebounds to the back wall before it strikes the floor.

Masters: In singles competition for players over 40; in doubles competition, one player must be at least 40, and his partner, at least 45.

Nonfront serve: A serve that hits any surface other than the front wall before hitting the front wall. This serve is illegal, and the penalty is loss of service.

Off-speed drive: A drive shot hit at medium speed, used for change of pace.

Off-the-back-wall kill: A kill shot struck as the ball rebounds off the back wall. *See also* kill.

Offensive position: Approximately center court; the most desirable spot for offensive play.

Offensive shot: Shot designed to win rally.

One-on-two: Game with three players in which the server plays the other two for the entirety of the game.

Opened: Racquet head faces a side wall rather than the front wall.

Out: Loss of serve as a result of an illegal serve.

Overhand: A shot that is struck over your head.

Pass shot: Ball shot out of your opponent's reach.

Point: Unit of scoring; tally scored by a successful player. Only the server can score a point.

Point of contact: The exact spot at which the racquet strikes the ball.

Rally: The time during which the ball is kept in play.

Ready position: The stance taken as you wait for the serve.

Receiver: The person to whom the serve is hit.

Receiving line: That line five feet in back of the short line. The receiver may not cross the receiving line until the ball has been served.

Referee: The person who makes all judgment calls in tournament play.

Reverse cross-court serve: *See* Garfinkel serve.

Roadrunner: A player whose speciality is retreiving.

Safety hinder: Stoppage of play when further play could result in injury.

Scotch: *See* cross-court serve.

Seamless 558: The official ball for the game of racquetball. The standard ball is 2½ inches in diameter, weighs approximately 1.4 ounces, and, at 76°F., will bounce 67-72 inches high when dropped from a height of 100 inches.

Serve: The act of putting the ball in play.

Server: Player who puts the ball in play.

Serve return: The receiver's first shot after the ball has been served.

Service box: The area 18 inches from the side wall, in which the nonserving member of a doubles team stands with his back to the wall while his partner serves.

Service line: The line parallel to and 5 feet in front of the short line.

Service zone: The court area between the short line and the service line, in which the server must stand while serving.

Setup: A shot that is easily returned.

Shooters: Players who depend to a great degree on kill shots. *See also* kill.

Short line: Line halfway between and parallel to the front and back walls.

Short serve: Serve that fails to rebound beyond the short line. This serve is illegal, and two such serves in succession result in loss of service.

Short court: *See* front court.

Side wall-front wall kill: A kill shot that hits the side wall and rebounds to the front wall. *See also* kill.

Side-out: Loss of serve.

Singles: Game of two players, one against the other.

Skip ball: Ball that hits the floor before it reaches the front wall.

Skip-in: *See* skip ball.

Straight kill: A kill shot hit directly into the front wall. *See also* kill.

Thong: Strap attached to racquet and worn around player's wrist. The strap must be fastened securely in order to eliminate the possibility of the racquet's flying out of control.

Three-quarters one-quarter: Definition of court responsibilities in doubles: an imaginary line is drawn diagonally from one front corner to the opposite back corner.

Three-quarter speed drive: *See* off-speed drive.

Three-wall serve: Serve that hits three walls on fly; illegal.

Top spin: Rotation of the ball in a clockwise direction.

Trigger grip: Method of holding racquet as if it were a pistol.

Tournament play: Formal competitive play under scheduled conditions.

Turning point: The time during a game or match that is considered crucial.

Unavoidable hinder: Accidental interference with opponent or flight of ball. No penalty is suffered, and the rally is replayed.

Undercut: To put backspin on the ball.

Volley: *See* rally.

V pass shot: Passing shot in which the ball strikes first the front wall, then the side wall or near the short line, rebounding in V fashion away from or behind your opponent.

Wallpaper ball: A shot that hugs so close to a wall that it is extremely difficult to return.

Winners: Kill shots. *See also* kill.

Z ball: Shot that hits the front wall, the side wall, and then the opposite wall without striking the floor.

Z ball return: Z ball used as return of service.

Z serve: *See* cross-court serve.

index